A HANDBOOK

of

STELLAR MAGICK

ISBN 978 1 907881 71 8 (Hardback)
ISBN 978 1 907881 70 1 (Paperback)
ISBN 978 1 907881 72 5 (Digital)
A catalogue for this title is available from the British Library.
10 9 8 7 6 5 4 3 2 1

First published in 2017 by Hadean Press
West Yorkshire
England

WWW.HADEANPRESS.COM

A HANDBOOK

of

STELLAR MAGICK

Cath Thompson

For Jim

I must thank Richard, Will, and Davey
for their enduring help and support.
My gratitude to all those
Brothers and Sisters of the O∴A∴A∴
who gave permission for their Magickal Records
to be used in this book.

TABLE OF CONTENTS

FOREWORD

IT IS NOT my purpose here to teach astrology – there are plenty of opportunities available to the student for that – but to demonstrate the relevance of astrology to ritual Magick. I imagine that while most people with an interest in the occult will be aware of their Zodiac Sign, probably not so many will be familiar with their natal charts, and fewer still will be able to cast a chart and interpret it. Ritual and Astrology have become separated in the West since the days of Dr John Dee. Apart from some herbal traditions involving the phase of the Moon, and seasonal rites which by their very nature are astrologically timed albeit in a very simple fashion, there appears to have been a reduction and dilution of emphasis placed upon astrological synchronicity in European occultism. Indeed, following the heyday of the Great Revival, Ritual magick and Astrology seem to have arrived at the 21st Century in different carriages, and the astrologer has acquired a degree of respectability which the ceremonial magickian knows not. The general principles of magickal astrology have not been formulated, until now.

The present work is the result of nearly half a century of practical research and sheer hard work by the membership of the O.'.A.'.A.'. under the leadership of

James Lees (Brother Leo), work both theoretical and practical which continued after his death in 2015. This book is a unique and definitive study of Astrological Magick, the only account of this coherent and infallible system, which is as easily practised by the experienced ritualist with full Temple regalia as by the most ignorant and naive neophyte with nothing more than a Tarot pack, and an East facing windowsill for an Altar.

Here is outlined the Royal Art to which present-day astrology is but the shadow to the torch. We describe the symbolism and use of Stellar Magick, explain the true meanings and powers of the astrological phenomena, and detail the requirements for the performance of the Stellar ritual. Here too we give details of the philosophy of the Stellar Science, illustrate its all-embracing completeness, and demonstrate its relevance to modern humanity. Most importantly we include a set of planetary invocations and formulae for all the beneficial astrological rites, with instructions for the manufacture and consecration of the planetary talismans and weapons, and accounts of our own personal experiences and results from our continuous practice of this system.

The stars which governed the writing of this grimoire also rule its present and future readership and their use of our information. All that needs to be said is – Try it. We have examined the past and predicted the future – it is for you to devise your own experiments. But the answers are most certainly there to be found, revealed in the stars and the forces which flow from them, in the planets which are the mundane Chakras of the Gods, and in the fixed Stars and constellations through which they eternally move. When you find that astrologically timed rituals do work, it is for you to begin to live and be truly aware of what you are and where your secret place is in the ever-changing cycles of the Universe, and maybe to come to know at last the true nature of the Gods themselves. For their powers exist and manifest in the divinity of mankind and reveal the truth about YOU. You are the embodiment of the Stellar configurations at the time of your birth – whether you accept it or not, your astrological birth chart is the portrait of your existence. You are indeed a Child of the Stars. It is you and your children who will establish the Golden Age on Earth.

1. THEORY

The basic principles of astrology, a fable of astrology's birth, modern astrology, the awakening of the celestial Sleeping Beauty, the activity of the Stellar Magickian, the importance of timing, useful astrological configurations, the Sun-Venus, the 418 Quaternary, a short study of Pluto in 418, Alchemy, the Part of Fortune, how Brother Leo came to write the rituals.

THE BASIC PRINCIPLES OF ASTROLOGY

LET US REMIND ourselves of the basic principles of astrology, and then attempt to examine its origins in the dawn of prehistory, and describe in some detail the development of this ancient and most royal art.

- As a baby will have the life ordained in the moment of birth, so anything begun at a particular time will have the characteristics and destiny of that moment.
- Everything that lives is a pioneer in time, an explorer in unknown territory.
- Nobody has existed in this time before.
- Each individual is exploring time anew.
- Humanity is born to explore his own particular time-span. It is not like anyone else's experience. The individual's experience of time will be uniquely his own. Some of the rules of time he will know: puberty, adolescence, adulthood, middle and old age are some of the signposts; but by far the majority of what is going to happen to him will be a mystery.

Man has devised many magical systems to try and make life more comprehensible and more understandable. He has attempted to make more and more elaborate maps of the unknown territory of Time. There are numerous systems of divination, but all are merely props to the insecurity of the pioneer of Time.

To the modern man this pioneering through the medium of time largely consists of careering from one blunder to another. Everything is new to him; there are no parameters as there were of old, religion is dead, modern philosophy is meaningless. Yet amid all this chaos there is a glimmer of meaning, a strange but coherent light from the mists of prehistory.

A FABLE OF ASTROLOGY'S BIRTH

ANCIENT MAN WAS not the fool that modern man is. He had the courage and honesty to face up to the insecurities of life, and he made some attempt to deal with them and face his destiny head on. Somehow, perhaps by trial and error over many centuries of observation and study, experiment, deduction, analysis, and synthesis, he learned that his life was not meaningless. He learned that there was a pattern to be discerned from his pioneering work through Time, and he came to understand that there was a relationship between all things celestial and terrestrial, that with the changing positions of the Sun, the Moon, and certain stars that did not twinkle much, there came parallel changes upon the earth. He began to record the changes in stellar relationships and the synchronous events upon the earth, until he had a considerable wealth of data for this primitive stellar science.

The first cycle that our hypothetical primitive man noticed was the menstrual cycle of his mate. He noticed that as the Moon moved through the sky, it gave rise to different moods in his woman. Early man was a little short on entertainment at night; apart from the Moon, the Stars and his woman, there was little going on. It was by no great feat of intellect that he noticed a correlation between the position of the Moon against its background of stars, and the changing humour of the one most important to him – his woman.

His interest would have been aroused by the fact that every time the Moon was in a particular constellation, his woman bled. This would have been magical to him. He would have been utterly amazed that this creature could affect the Moon's position. He would not have made the assumptions we do today, and think that the Moon's cycle merely coincided with the menstrual cycle. His assumption would be different; he would link his woman with the Stars and assume some form of relationship.

So here we have a man noticing his woman linked in with those mysterious points of light in the sky. In a spirit of scientific interest he decides to see if there is any other relationships between this strange creature who bears his children – already he is in awe of her on that score alone – and lunar and Stellar phenomena. He notices that as the Moon waxes and wanes through the Zodiac her moods change. He has nothing better to do, so he makes a note of the changes – it is a fascinating study. He finds his mate and the Stars playing out a sequence of events he can relate to. To him she has become a clock; she is magical. Perhaps he begins to realise that after thirteen of these bleeds Spring comes around again, and it would dawn on him that the Sun also follows this female cycle – except instead of the flow of blood, the leaves fall off the trees and it becomes cold.

He begins to see all kinds of relationships between his woman and the whole of nature around him; he concludes that Nature and the Stars must be female.

A HANDBOOK OF STELLAR MAGICK

He becomes the wise man of his tribe – after all, he has the edge on them, he can predict when spring is going to be, indeed he knows when all the seasons will occur; he is becoming a very important man indeed. He may not be the strongest man in the tribe, but he is the wisest. His knowledge has given him great stock with his neighbours. He studies his embryo astrology still further; he makes agricultural calendars based on the position of the Sun and Moon. Everything is magic, there is very little separation between his individual consciousness and his environment. The Spirits of his ancestors are probably never far away.

It is extremely unlikely that he placed any emphasis on the accumulation of personal wealth, or harboured notions of guilt and shame; he would however had lived with a much more intimate knowledge of death, and lived in preparation for the experience of discorporating and joining the ancestors.

When he begins observing and interpreting the appearances and interplay of certain stars which move across the night sky in regular slow patterns, becoming familiar with what we might call the planetary archetypes, he begins to build permanent places from which to study and propitiate and eventually worship. Perhaps he found planetary spirits living in the same abodes and accessible by similar art; he teaches his children, and subsequent generations develop the Art still further until it becomes institutionalised as religion.

From these tentative and tender beginnings the whole Art of Astrology depends. Now this may only be a flight of fancy, but this story of evolutionary development might be easier to accept than the allegory of Athene Goddess of Wisdom springing all at once and fully formed from the mind of the God. It seems extremely unlikely that we will ever know any real truth about humanity's prehistoric past, and equally unwise to make assumptions about it.

Our primitive astrologer would have found that the stars concealed living archetypes or Gods that could be propitiated by the right course of action, and moreover that different physical substances – such as plants, stones, animals, etc. – could act as storehouses for the various astral forces that surrounded him, and so the art of making talismans was born. He learned that if he manufactured a talisman when the stars were propitious his future became more fortunate. He found that by his knowledge of the correspondences between terrestrial and celestial phenomena, he could influence and propitiate these celestial entities that ruled men's lives. The magician was born, the leader of the tribe. This was the man or woman who could read the stars and by sympathetic magic influence and propitiate the Gods that the stars concealed, and thus make the tribe's passage through time more secure. Make no mistake about it, this magician of old was no con man. He knew what he was doing. He understood the universal character of the experience of Time. A man's life depended upon the directives of his magician King, and if the prognostications delivered by the King turned out to be inaccurate then that King was sacrificed to the Gods and another, more effective magician reigned. If the magician-King was to survive he had to be good!

In the prehistoric past, the past of pyramids, straight tracks, and standing stones, man lived in a harmonious universe, where everything was interrelated by magical ideas and interdependent by necessity. Time was a much more intimate mystery to him; he dealt with it using his magical philosophy. He invoked the Gods to make his future secure.

Ancient man's mode of mentation was nothing like ours. To him, half hallucinated by diet and experience, the world was a much more intimate place. Through vision he understood the curious subtle connections between things, the intricate web of relationships that seems utterly lost to modern man.

From these early beginnings (or something very like) came the great edifice of Magic that ruled men's lives for thousands of years. The magical view of life survived not because of the naivety of ancient man but because of his sophistication – anyone who may doubt this should go and try to find the man alive today who can REALLY explain how the pyramids were built. That mystery is a testament to the celestial and geocentric accuracy of the understanding possessed by their builders.

Ancient man was no fool; his magic worked, and through his magic he lived in harmony with the world around him, with no sense of separation between himself and that world. This magic that explained our ancestor to himself became a comprehensive and coherent way of life based upon the realities of his experience.

Our ancestors knew that if they did certain things at certain times, results would follow that would be consistent with their desires. The early pioneers of Time knew that for any project to succeed it must be started at the right time with the right ceremony. It was not enough to choose the right moment, the ceremony also was needed.

Let us explain this in more detail. Suppose you want to catch a train. The train will be standing at the station at a specific time, just as the planets are in aspect at specific times, so you know when to be there to get on board. But to use the train you have to go through the ceremony of buying a ticket, or you will not be allowed on the train. The same is true of Stellar magic – without the ceremony you will be unable to take advantage of stellar configurations and you will simply remain a victim of them.

From their observations of the Stars, the Ancients knew that these powers of the Zodiac and planets could be influenced by man, and that they were intelligent forces. These phenomena ceased to be seen merely as objects that moved in the heavens, but were recognised as reflecting vessels of the natures of the Gods and Goddesses themselves. The Planets and their relationships to each other became indicators of the relationships between the Deities. If the relationship was a good one then this would be a good time for beginning something that reflected the natures of the planets concerned. Thus when the Sun was conjunct Jupiter it would be a good time to start anything that represented health, wealth, and prosperity, in regal proportions. If Venus was in good aspect to the Sun then it would be a good time to begin events that were characterised by love, beauty, or great art. The beginning of anything important was celebrated by astrological ritual as this was the sure way of producing success in any enterprise, and that is true now as it was then. The Sun, Moon, and planets are the concrete representations or Mundane Chakras of Archetypal powers, the Gods and the Goddesses. In the interplay of the planets is a cosmic adjustment of the earth so that life continues to exist. The movement of the celestial bodies and their influence upon the Earth and its inhabitants is literally the Will of God in action.

MODERN ASTROLOGY

CONSIDER THE PROPOSITION implied in a complete interpretation of an individual's natal chart. The astrologer will read therein not only the personal characteristics of the individual, but also those of his parents, his children, his spouse, and his employers, and his relationships with them all. Traumas, accidents, criminal tendencies, home environment, good and bad fortune, employment, changes in the preferred lifestyle, births, marriages, and deaths, all are predictable from a careful study of the nativity, which inevitably gives rise to the transcendent idea of the unity of all humanity whether past, present, or future. The reasoning mind will object until it is overwhelmed by the logic of the proposition.

Modern astrology is a blurred remnant of a Golden Age whose passing was witnessed by the pharaohs, and yet the passage of Time has not adulterated its truth nor impoverished its symbolism. The use of astrology for the interpretation of an individual's nativity is and always has been but an offshoot of this royal art. Astrology conceals a magically sophisticated way of life, a life in harmony with the world and the cosmos. The true purpose of astrology in the great civilisations of the past was to predict the right time for the beginning of any undertaking, from the quarrying of the first blocks of stone for the building of temples and great cities to the grinding of pigments for their embellishment, from the preparation of sacred incenses to the conception of a child.

The planets, Zodiac, and associated symbols reflect the history of mankind. As each new planet or relationship is discovered or rediscovered, a parallel factor in the nature of humanity is isolated. With the discoveries of Neptune, Uranus, and Pluto, there came on a reawakening of the transcendental nature in man and woman. With each new planet there came several new factors. Neptune gave us the mystic defined, and Uranus the magician. With Pluto we have the unity of these two approaches, the Stellar magickian.

Astrology is magic and magic has always had its roots in astrology. Some modern astrologers have attempted to divorce astrology from magic and have tried to align its concepts with more primitive systems such as psychology. The results have been unsuccessful. Freud's man is based on sex, Jung's is all about individuation, and then there is Adler's Power-Complex, and all the rest – none of these are able to encompass the infinite and kaleidoscopic variations of the human psyche, which a competent astrologer is able to delineate on a day-to-day basis.

No! Astrology when applied to the soul reveals it clear and transparent without the bias of man's personal ignorance. It needs no props, it does not require hedging about with absurd modernistic half-baked and ill-tested notions. It is centuries older than the recorded history of mankind. Astrology stands alone

A HANDBOOK OF STELLAR MAGICK

and complete; its signposts on the road to the Truth indicate a Golden Age of total integrity. It is and always has been the Royal Art, and its practitioners should be capable of accepting, without bias or preconceived ideas, that it needs not the comfort of fitting in with modern fads and fancies.

THE AWAKENING OF THE
CELESTIAL SLEEPING BEAUTY

ASTROLOGY WORKS UPON the principle of "Anything born of a moment of time has the quality of that moment of time". Stellar magick partakes of the same principle. If one takes a course of action that is symbolically consistent with the Stellar configurations of the time, one can imitate the process of birth and alter the future in accordance with one's Will.

Recent developments in particle physics have found that in the moment that a particle is "born" it explores time and space backward and forward before moving forward in linear time to fulfill its function in manifestation. It is precisely this moment when time literally stands still that is the province of the Stellar magickian because it is in this moment that he can cause changes to occur in the future.

The configurations of the planets are moments of birth in which the particle or idea that is born is defined by the astrological natures of the planets involved. This new beginning is a birth that reverberates throughout the Solar system, and if the magician catches this moment he can influence the future in accordance with the nature of the planets involved.

Science has also shown that the earth is bathed in two subtle forms of energy known as the Solar Wind and the Galactic Wind, which apparently wax and wane over extended periods of time. When the Solar Wind is predominant, as it has been for the last 2000 years or so, it protects the earth from Stellar influences and humanity's awareness of the Stellar deities becomes dimmed and obscured as the power of the Solar deities prevails. It is just a simple fact, and it is futile to point accusing fingers of blame into history's conquests and triumphs and defeats and massacres, for we do not know the whole story.

We can assess the available evidence however, and it seems clear that the influence of the Solar deities is diminishing and the Galactic or Stellar powers are once more making their presence felt in human consciousness. People are born with more clearly defined astrological characteristics than in previous generations. The discovery of Pluto in 1930 was a significant marker in Time; the transformation of the human collective can be traced back to the entrance of the Dwarf-God into the Golden Temple of the Zodiac, and as usual the worst effects came first, ruthlessly violent and destructive on a global scale. It may take some time for everybody to settle down in the New Aeon, but make no mistake, Pluto came as the Herald of the Goddess of the Stars, and She is waking up fast at the beginning of the 21ˢᵗ Century.

The new cosmological factors in human consciousness were first apprehended by intelligent sensitive women, daughters of the Star Goddess, who were often subjected to all sorts of deleterious treatment as their menfolk tried to suppress the perceived threat in the awakening nature of Woman, and to stave off their own apprehension and anxiety experienced as a result of the unrecognised and awakened Stellar influence upon their minds.

The freeing of woman from the dominion of man is an allegory of the awakening Goddess. The actual liberation of woman from man is an absurd concept; it is perhaps brutal, but honest, to admit the fact that man plays an indispensable role in a woman's life, quite apart from the biological necessities of sex and reproduction. It is man who shows woman her transcendental nature. Woman can cleanse woman of the accretions of male dominated history, but ultimately she is only being prepared as a bride, for the "new man"; and the emancipated woman knows this.

This is no male chauvinistic arrogance, but a simple fact. Woman is prepared by woman and that is a fact of nature which is reflected in every marriage preparation of every religion. What has been lost and forgotten is that woman was prepared in the ways of the Goddess. She was initiated into the mysteries of the Goddess. She became a being proud in her nature, conscious of her possibilities, and it became her husband's task upon marriage to explain her to herself, so that she could transcend her negative femininity and have a positive point of view. That point of view culminated in a child of the marriage, physical or magical.

The husband in his love and sympathy of his wife transcends his brutish masculinity and comes to understand nature through her. The more man understands woman, the more he understands nature. Nature, the Goddess, refines man, makes him aware of philosophy, the arts, and initiates the Quest through his love for Her – the quest for truth through love, not as at present the quest for truth through pure curiosity. Woman reflects nature; if man can understand her he is initiated into the true mystery of his masculinity and he will lose that sense of inadequacy that is the ultimate experience of male dominated religions and systems, that sense of inadequacy which all gods of war and destruction hold dear to their hearts, and which manipulates men to their own destruction.

Everyone who reads an astrology book is unconsciously worshipping and awakening the Stellar Gods. Everyone who casts a Horoscope or reads a chart is contributing to the awakening power of the Stars. The age of the Stellar Goddess is upon us now, the Sleeping Beauty awakens with her seven Dwarves clustering around Her, and slowly but surely the Art and Science of Astrology will become more and more prominent in the general consciousness.

THE ACTIVITY OF THE STELLAR MAGICKIAN

THE INVOCATION AND use of planetary forces does not result in an idolatrous religion, but having all the known attributes of God and Goddess as indicated by the stars, the magickian is enabled to take the Gnostic leap from what is known (i.e. the Zodiac and so forth) to what is unknown, that is, the transcendental nature of himself and God. By continually working Stellar magick the magickian eventually transcends the known and explicable to the unknown and the divine. Human consciousness enhanced and refined by the use of Stellar Ritual can and does attain true cosmic consciousness.

From the point of view of Astrology all life is seen as ritual, in that all things can be predicted by astrology. The Stellar Magickian sees life as ritual, and seeks to enhance the positive attributes and minimise the negative. This he does by the practice of astrologically based magical rituals performed at the astrologically correct time, that is to say, when the planets are in good aspect to each other, and preferably positioned in the most conducive Zodiac Signs. He uses particular planets for different purposes; thus he propitiates Venus for matters of love, Mars for energy, Jupiter for good fortune and good fellowship, and so on.

The student would do well to learn the basics of divinatory or Horary Astrology, for it is most closely allied to the practice of Stellar Magick. A Horary Chart is drawn for the moment of asking a question, which usually follows an event which has provoked the enquiry. The interpretation can be a simple "Yes" or "No" reading, or with a little practice a deeper elucidation may be gained regarding the sequence of events and the length of time required for the resolution of the question to be completed. Since the onset of the computer age most astrologically minded occultists will simply put the chart up on the screen, which is much easier than taking pen, paper, and ephemeris, and doing calculations involving sidereal times and degrees of longitude; but the Stellar Magickian will nevertheless draw the chart up on paper or other material if it is appropriate to do so, for it is also a talisman of the moment and the celestial forces at work and play in that moment.

In the event of an individual requiring the assistance of a Stellar Magickian for whatever reason, the magickian erects a chart to find out what the prevailing influences are at the moment when the Question is received and understood by him. This is the birth-moment of the idea and the chart will reflect it and show the magickian the forces that are at work in the situation at hand. If the auguries are good he will go no further, but if they are not then he will use his magick to change future events in line with the requirements of his client.

As an example, when a man comes along and asks whether it is possible that he will obtain a particular job, a chart is erected for the moment and if it shows affirmation by good relationships between the First House (the client) and the Tenth House (the prospective employer) then the matter can end there; there is nothing more to be done. Conversely if the chart shows failure, the magickian chooses a time when the Stars are helpful, and constructs and performs a ritual consistent with his client's requirements. He will then cast another chart to see if the Company of Heaven has been influenced by his efforts.

Finding the right time is done by searching the Zodiac for configurations that are consistent with the wishes of the client. This process is a very technical one, and some years experience of the art would be required of anyone wishing to take up this particular branch of Astrology. The reason for this is twofold: firstly he must have the astro-magical knowledge; but at the same time he must have the initiation necessary to complete the work, that is he must be "accepted" by the Gods as a true worshipper of the Stellar Goddess. Assuming he fulfills the conditions, the Magickian can go to work and having found the stellar requirements of his client, he will construct his ritual to "capture" the coming influences. The ritual is performed at the correct astrological time and the results awaited.

Should the Stars prove beneficial he instructs his client that nothing more need be done and explains how the matter will come to pass by interpreting the chart. Should it be that for some reason his invocations have failed he will continue until such time that the Stars comply with his demands.

If the magickian has any skill at all he should be able to deal with the problem relatively quickly. The only exception to the rule is when there are definite Karmic indications shown by the birth chart that the individual should suffer some kind of privation that precludes him from achieving his desire. Even in this case the magickian should be able to fulfill his client's will, but he should warn him that he has caused a stress in the Astral and it may "bounce back" and cause him to lose what he has gained when the powers invoked by the magickian begin to mutate, due to the nature of Time.

There is a factor that we have not mentioned hitherto, and that factor is synchronicity. The client comes to the Stellar magickian synchronistically, and the magickian acts simply as a catalyst that causes the change to occur. We heard of a case some years ago involving a wife who had gone off with "the love of her life" and the magickian had great difficulty in getting her back for his client. It took three separate rituals to bring back the erring lady, but back she came, and bang on time too, according to the predictions of the chart. However, they had lost their house and all the possessions of their marriage, and the final result was an amicable divorce some time later.

By taking advantage of an astrological aspect such as Moon conjunct Venus where the Moon governs everyday events and Venus is the Goddess of love, one can make any woman subject to one's will, by contacting the force and mediating it by magickal ritual. In actual practice the Stellar magickian simply invokes the Star Gods and Goddesses at the most astrologically propitious moment by an act of worship. By doing this he ensures that they will aid him in all circumstances.

He only really concerns himself with specific cases when he is acting on behalf of another person who is not privy to the secrets of his art.

The "vitalising" of an astrological chart is one of the great secrets of magick, but it is perfectly simple with just one prerequisite. The magickian must be initiated. That means he must have gone through an astrologically based process that has taught him the special integrity that is an absolute essential; for he must be found worthy by the Gods before he can attempt such work. Many and varied are the ways in which the Stellar magickian can influence the prevailing powers, it all depends upon his skill and experience, but most of all his success depends upon his degree of initiation, that is to say to what extent he can mediate the planetary powers within himself, and this in turn depends upon whether he has been favoured by the planetary deities with the power to mediate their influences.

It is up to each individual Stellar magickian to make the contact with the Gods, and it is not as difficult as you might think. The dead-letter approach to the science of the Stars is at an end. The Stellar Art is a way of life when one awakens and the Eye of Shiva opens. Whereas once it was difficult to open this Eye, calling for years of Yoga discipline, now it is relatively easy. One has merely to practise the rituals, and invoke the Gods to aid one in one's daily life. Practise the magick of the Stars, for with continued practice comes awareness, and with that awareness comes knowledge, with knowledge comes integrity and with integrity comes the vision of the One that exists in the All. There is no suffering in our philosophy, no pain that has not been engendered in past incarnations by our foolish acts – acts which have been committed in our blindness. The practise of Stellar Magick removes the blindness.

To illustrate this, the results generally agreed upon by the O.'.A.'.A.'. members at the end of the 1970s and after early experimental performances of a Jupiter ritual were as follows:

"An increase in awareness including an enhanced telepathic consciousness of where the different members of the group are and their general state of mind. A personal feeling of oneness with the Will of God. People become more friendly towards one. A sense from other people that one is not like them. They begin by reacting in the normal way, look puzzled for a second or two and then suddenly, almost with surprise and a sense of relief 'open up' and reveal their real selves, their anxieties and worries; as if unconsciously they are aware that we can somehow, by their talking to us, relieve them of their worries. We feel that by simply listening to them we can help by absorbing their problems into the greatness of Jupiter. There is no effort in this. All one has to do is 'be' in the ambience of the God, and all will be resolved for ourselves and the people we meet.

"By the continual practice of the worship of the Stellar deities one is brought closer and closer to the Will of God. What once were ideas and symbols become living realities. One looks at the images of the Gods and Goddesses of the Stars expecting them to be dead symbols and suddenly with surprise we see them alive as entities so close to us that we simply could not see them before. Jupiter, that grand benign magnificent

God, has always been there, and now we see him in all his living glory."

It comes as quite a shock at first, as the change from dead symbol to living entity is sudden and uncalled for. The power and image of the God is with us in daily life, there to be communicated with directly. There is a constant awareness of the Stellar deities as living entities. Each one is filled with a different kind of love. The love that Jupiter radiates is benign and at the same time positive. He appears as a middle-aged King and sometimes as a wise man. When as a King he is robed and crowned in all purple and gold, as a wise man his colours become a little subdued and his robes more conservative, but all the while there is the knowledge, the awareness that he is alive.

How can one see the Gods? It is not quite with the mind's eye and it is definitely not imagination, because the vision intrudes uninvited and in brilliant colours. One has the awareness that one can contact them directly at all times. The mind itself has "changed gear" as it were, and one is not what one was. After performing a handful of Stellar rituals one member wrote,

"One moment I am alone in the Universe, without aid of any kind and the next moment I am surrounded by a knowledge, a gnosis. A knowing for myself how vastly alive is the Universe and how real these entities are.

"At first I am a little perplexed, how can it be, that by simply invoking these powers in an act of worship, they should come to me? It doesn't work with any other system. Religions demand that one has to have faith, endless faith, in a god that may or may not exist. There is no proof of him, but the proof of the Astrological deities is immediate in their power to influence one through the practice of the art; but the step beyond, from accepting them as dead-letter symbols that have an effect upon our lives and nothing more, to realising them as living changing entities, bent on assisting mankind in general and oneself in particular, is an amazing experience.

"One has actually contacted something beyond oneself that lives on a plane beyond oneself in a greatness that is not remote, but is so intimate that one is a part of It and It is a part of oneself, all at the same time.

"As one continues to invoke these powers when their planets are favourably placed, so one increases in intimacy with them and their purpose. There begins to form a bond of love between oneself and these powers, Gods, or whatever one likes to call them; and with the continued worship of the Stellar deities comes another awareness, an awareness of something beyond them, dimly perceived at first but growing stronger. It is an awareness of what the Stellar deities are not, a kind of power that does not depend on their existence, but transcends them.

"I was puzzled by this at first, but the more I worshipped the Stellar Gods, the more I became aware of this other, greater power that transcended them, and I began to be aware of its nature. It was the informing power of all the Gods, their source and inspiration. It was superior to the Gods and yet informed them and permeated them, it was one with them and yet apart. I began to concentrate upon this power, its influence seemed so strong.

"I became aware that it was the Will of God, the Will that informed all the Gods and Goddesses of the Stars. I became aware, with an intimacy that astounded me, that the Stellar deities were the Will of God in action. Each in its different way was expressing the Will of God, each was and is influencing mankind from moment to moment throughout eternity.

"It was as if I was the Sleeping Beauty, who had suddenly awakened from a long sleep, because my previous consciousness seemed like a dream-state. I had only been half alive, I had been aware of nothing beyond the mechanistic pointless world of the twentieth century, and I was now plunged into a reality far more real than the dream I had been dreaming. Who or what was the "Prince" that had awakened me? Was it the Gods themselves that had drawn me to this Place? I felt that I had been gently guided to this mystery but it didn't matter, the fact was that I was awake at last. Through the Stellar deities I can see the meaning, purpose, and magnificence of life."

Some twenty years later another Initiate wrote, "When I started out with Stellar Magick I just printed off the rituals, and gave it a try. *How can this work?* I thought, such was my ignorance back then, but work it did, and with great results. I walked into another realm that lay just beyond an invisible curtain and I have never looked back. Mind-blowingly effective are these rituals, and delightful in their simplicity."

It has also been observed that repeated performance of Stellar Magick rituals often results in an accumulation of Astral phenomena in the immediate environment, which may become visible to domestic pets, and to the uninitiated but sensitive visitor. One individual who was staying in the home of an Initiate remarked that after a few days, "I began to witness curious strange light anomalies. I first noticed brief flashes of light – sometimes oval shaped – suddenly and unexpectedly appear and vanish whilst I was sitting alone in the living room. My initial reaction was that it may be reflections from the street, but they increased in presence and became less easily explainable.

"One evening I had an apparition of a spear of light manifesting directly in front of me. A golden rod about four feet long just appeared and then in a moment was gone! It was apparent that all was not as it seemed around my friend's home; and somewhat in a state of shock, I approached him for explanations. He was incredibly calm in his response and sat me down and explained that he engaged in something known as 'Stellar Magick', based upon astrological correspondences. I had never come across anything like this before, I knew he was a keen and able astrologer, but rituals to planets and deities thereof seemed something from the history of a people from a bygone age. It never occurred to me that such traditions still existed, and I found that whilst some things became clearer to me, other greater questions began to form in my mind...

"I began having very profound dreams, of a place where symbols would appear and my friend would be teaching me meanings of them. I kept a journal, and began to see many synchronicities from my dreams into my waking life..."

This particular individual was initiated into the O∴A∴A∴ within two years of these events. It is almost a necessity to keep a journal of some sort if one is hoping to become a Stellar Magickian, to keep track of one's development and learn from one's mistakes.

THE IMPORTANCE OF TIMING

EVERYTHING HAS ITS proper time and season and ritual magick is no exception to this. Indeed, the critical factor in the performance of any practical magick is the timing. For example, in the case of an event synchronised with a dynamic Mercury-Venus-Jupiter, success would very probably follow or at least everybody would have a good time, but synchronising with a malefic Mars-Saturn influence would guarantee a flat and turgid event, and travelling to and fro would not be straightforward. Of course these effects may pass unremarked by those insensitive to such phenomena, but in the case of magickal ritual the initiates should certainly be sufficiently switched on to feel the impact of the Stellar forces combining in an astrological aspect, even if they are not directly conscious of the fact.

It is most unwise to move into a new dwelling with the Moon in Scorpio, (or indeed to start any new undertaking at that time), but to take up residence in new surroundings under a Venus trine Jupiter will bring good fortune and happiness. This happened to a lady of our acquaintance, who did the Moon-Scorpio move and experienced a run of bad luck which resulted in another move, this time into a two-room mobile home. It was pitched on a site with fifty others, and the site owners decided to move her home from one end of the site to the other. They fixed the date, and she was overjoyed when she consulted her ephemeris and found a favourable Venus-Jupiter the next day. She lived there very happily for several years, and finally departed to move into a house, on another Venus-Jupiter. It had been left by the vendors in immaculate condition, decorated throughout in shades of green, blue, and purple, the colours of Venus and Jupiter, with no Martial red anywhere. These sorts of synchronicities tend to happen to Stellar Magickians. We know of a couple who regularly walk across a three way junction with multiple traffic lights without breaking stride as all the lights change and the vehicles stop like a mechanised Red Sea, and they divine their interconnectedness with the Universe accordingly.

Many gardeners will plant their seeds on a new moon, many religious festivals are synchronised with lunar phases, even though the meaning of the symbolism is long lost. The Stellar magickian navigates through Time and picks up the favourable currents that he knows how to find and take on the flood. He knows too that there are ebb tides and slack waters and flat calm periods; and also, naturally, there are turbulent stormy times when great care must be exercised.

We have remarked that Time can behave in a non-linear fashion, as event-moments ripple backwards from the future as well as forwards. For example, a good Sun-Jupiter with a lunar aspect to mediate the harmonised forces of the Gods, is noted by the Stellar magickian a fortnight in advance. As soon as that future event impinges upon his mind and he in turn reaches forward to it in anticipation, that is to say, with magickal intent, a marker has been placed on that moment in time. There may be many reasons why he will not take it up as he comes alongside it in the future, in which case the idea of a ritual will bear no fruit and the moment will be more or less unremarkable, but if there is to be a ritual then the energy of the marker will increase as it radiates from the event-moment, according to the skill of the magickian, until the whole period leading up to the date in question will bear the characteristics of the moment.

One young Adept, accustomed to this phenomenon, had fixed a date for a ritual and was observing the effects coming back to him, but there seemed to be something awry and all was not as he would have expected. The event was a Mercury sextile Mars with the last lunar aspect being a conjunction with Mercury, all on the day of the Summer Solstice. The initial plan was to invoke both planetary deities, and celebrate with an appropriate feast afterwards. However, as the appointed day drew near, much anxiety about the ritual was noted and the atmosphere became very edgy and disharmonious. To quote wholesale from his Record:

"Two days before the ritual, a sly-looking workman visited the house to do some electrical repairs. We apprehended him sneaking into the bedroom where we suspected he was about to steal something. A horary chart backed up this hunch and I saw it as a bad omen in regards to our intended invocation of Mercury.

"On the day before the ritual, the mood was intensely heavy and there was perhaps the greatest amount of resistance to performing a ritual that I had ever encountered. Upon reading the ephemeris again I noticed that Mercury was exactly in square aspect to Saturn just hours before our proposed ritual. How could I have missed this configuration? The horary regarding the thieving workman had been a big overlooked warning. The preposterousness of invoking Mercury whilst he was squared Saturn makes me chuckle even now; and certainly explained having a potential thief in the house, and the prevailing atmosphere of miscommunication. We agreed not to invoke the afflicted Mercury and to make the ritual entirely about Mars, using him to express the dynamic energy of the Summer Solstice.

"Upon making this decision my mood lightened and four magpies (very much Mercury/Saturn creatures) that recently had been driving me mad with their incessant cackling in the tree outside, instantly flew away. The sun also came out and we were both glad that we had been made aware of the negatively aspected Mercury; but even after the decision was made to drop Mercury from the proceedings the day was still one of antagonism and discord. The build up to the Mars ritual was very trying indeed, with much resistance, trepidation and concern. We decided to perform the ritual with Mars in the Ninth House, a weaker house than the Seventh which we had initially decided upon. A cautionary minimising of the possible impact by moving the House sat well with both of us.

"There is little recollection to convey of the ritual itself except for the hot and masculine atmosphere and the redness of everything amidst the billowing and raw plumes of Dragon's Blood incense. Proceedings all went very smoothly during the rite but as is usually the case the details vanished upon departing the temple, leaving just a feeling of success and victory and that the ritual had been powerful. We were aware that we had both been transported somewhere else for the duration.

"Post-ritual we feasted in honour of Mars and all was very masculine and abounding with comradery. There was the feeling that we had returned from battle victorious and were celebrating our triumphant homecoming. Our toasts of champagne were like battle toasts, spoken with passion and violently fighting for justice. We had the notion of brutally slaying demons, and felt we should have been wearing armour, helmets and chain-mail.

"Little appetite was present at first but much force and vigour of conversation was evident. Such a feeling of victory and triumph. The whole of our feasting quarters was adorned with red and the evening became very boisterous. The red velvet tablecloth bore the scars of our evening and emerged war-torn, burnt and battered after the feast, which continued with boisterous merriment until 4 am.

"The darkness and disharmony had been totally eradicated (slain even) and was replaced with a very dynamic energy. Prior to the ritual there had been an onrush of Mars in a destructive potency, and post ritual it had balanced itself out and felt constructive. The following days found me with a strong feeling of confidence and heightened sexual energy. A certain martial boldness in its most dignified sense, yet also with a certain destructive clumsiness that saw items smashed and appendages burnt, all of it in good humour. The television would turn itself on and up in the early hours of the morning, cups flew out of cupboards unaided and we found great humour in the activities of the mischievous spirits of Mars (in aspect with Mercury and the Moon).

"The feeling of being noble warriors continued and external manifestations amused us day by day. One of the more memorable of these was waking up to a giant conifer (which neither of us liked by the house) being cut down and chipped by a horrendously noisy machine just outside our window. Another amusing manifestation was in relation to our dog Eric, dogs being under the jurisdiction of Mars. A poster of a dog wearing a crown and looking exactly like Eric appeared by our front door. This coincided with Eric's behaviour becoming quite unruly, and receiving a present of a huge basket of dog-food from our neighbour, whose much older dog had died recently. A gift from Mars as it were, as the God took the life of a weaker animal to bring our Eric great fortune.

"We also started receiving much respect from martial men who were suddenly more prominent in our lives. The rapport with our Butcher went off the scale!

"The dynamic energy of Mars stayed with me and integrated beautifully into my psyche and I went forward with an increased sense of masculine confidence that I now realise had been lacking in its vigour prior to this rite."

USEFUL ASTROLOGICAL CONFIGURATIONS

THE PLANETS MOST useful to the Stellar Magickian are the ones that he can see moving across the sky, the traditional seven comprising Sun, Moon, Mercury, Venus, Mars, Jupiter, and Saturn. Saturn is rarely invoked, as his tendency to solidify and crystallise and generally slow everything down is not desirable. His spirits are notoriously difficult to get rid of, and all astrology reckons him a malefic influence. For that very reason though he must not be overlooked.

Mercury bestows swiftness and accuracy and is useful for aid with matters of communication and writing. Venus is of course the Goddess of Love, and she has governance of the inspirational Muses; she is invoked for all matters of romance, beauty, harmony, and artistic creativity. Mars however is all energy and activity and although easy to invoke, he should be approached with respect and caution as he readily tends towards destruction, and his spirits can be hard to banish. Jupiter, the largest of the planets, is the most generous; called the Bringer of Joy, he gives good fortune, happiness, abundance, wealth and prosperity.

Harmonious aspects with the luminaries, the Sun and the Moon, vitalise and empower the planetary deities. The Sun's influence is used to affect general events and background atmospheres while the Moon has a more direct effect upon day to day events. By experimental trial and error the O∴A∴A∴ ascertained that Solar conjunctions in Stellar Magick follow the same rule as in Horary, which is to say that the power of the Sun consumes the planetary influence for the period of the conjunction, and therefore the Stellar Magickian rarely works with a planet conjunct the Sun and would always look for a trine or even a sextile instead for the most harmonious combination of Stellar influences. The sextile is weaker than the trine in effect and duration of the harmony generated. Moon conjunct Sun should be avoided unless separating and in trine or sextile one or more planet; this is of course the New Moon, and it is better to have her waxing again than still waning. The Full Moon is in opposition to the Sun, and again it is better to have her coming up to being full than separating and beginning to lose light. This opposition is the only "bad" aspect that is any good to the Stellar Magickian.

The Sun in trine or sextile to one or more planet is utilised to generally bring the planetary influences more closely into the lives of the ritualists for a given occasion. Sun-Jupiter is ideal for banquets, Sun-Mercury for literary festivals, for example.

The Moon conjunct, trine, or sextile to one or more planets is invoked to focus the celestial forces more intimately for particular purposes, such as the creation of elixirs, construction of talismans, and blessings and consecrations of all kinds.

Two or more planets conjunct, trine, or sextile each other may be invoked by appointed officers who have identified themselves with their particular Deity, or by the individual who has had enough practical experience with planetary invocation to be able to mediate the different forces at will.

To begin with we would suggest a series of monthly rituals to celebrate a lunar aspect such as Moon conjunct Venus or Jupiter. These are the two great benefics of all astrology, and it is the beneficial effects of astrological influences that one is primarily interested in when one begins to work with this branch of the Art. As the beginner advances in the knowledge of magic, and when the magician has made his contacts with the powers behind the symbols, then and only then will he be allowed to deal with the more fast acting and direct forms of magickal work without the risk of burnt fingers.

The planets have particular affinities with the Signs of the Zodiac, which are known to astrologers as "dignities" and which enhance or weaken a planet's influence. The more dignity a planet has in the Sign the better, as far as the Stellar Magickian is concerned. For example, the best Sign in which to find the Moon is Taurus, where she is exalted, and her influence will be reflective of the most harmony and beauty. The Moon rules Cancer, and there she is strongest. Capricorn however is where the Moon is in her fall, and she is at her weakest. Over time the ritualised marking of the lunar position will sensitise the magickian so that he will know when she changes Sign, and where she is in her earthly orbit.

Conjunctions are active and dynamic mixtures of Stellar forces tempered by the characteristics of the

Zodiac Sign in which they are placed. Trines and sextiles are a bit more subtle but no less effective. In the event of a trine or sextile between two planets with the Moon going to conjunct one of them, she will obviously be aspecting the other as well, and when she is between the two she will be forming what is known as a midpoint. In this time period the Moon will reflect the powers of the two planets united in the compatibility of the aspect and she will transmit that harmony "without division or diminution". This movement between two or more aspecting planets is known as "translation of light" and naturally happens more frequently with the Moon than with the Sun.

The astrological division of the Heavens into the twelve Houses is of paramount importance in Stellar magick, particularly the Angles or Cardinal Points, which are the most dynamic. They are known as the First House, also called the Ascendant, which is the Eastern horizon and represents the Magickian. Due South and overhead is the Tenth House or Midheaven, which is the overseeing authority in the chart. On the Western horizon is the Seventh House representing alliances and partnerships pertaining to the Magickian, and the Fourth House is the North, the Earth below our feet and the Place of Greatest Darkness, wherein may be discovered the final result or end of the matter.

By paying attention to the timing of his rite the Magickian places his planetary deities in the House best suited to his purpose. Thus the Tenth House is used to get into contact with the spirit by means of worship. The planet in the Seventh is used when one requires the force to act upon one's behalf. The Fourth

House is used for casting spells, and the Ascendant is used when one wishes to embody the God involved, by the method of Assumption of the God-form. In each case the planet whose God is to be invoked and worshipped must be in the appropriate House, that which is most conducive to the magickian's work. In the case of a Solar aspect, having the Sun in the Tenth is ideal for worship, as it confers the supreme Authority upon the planet in question. For Rituals and Spells of the Seventh and Fourth we would require an applying conjunction with the Moon.

It is not always possible to have the planets in the right places. For general magickal work the planetary days and hours can be used when there are no astrological configurations available to aid one in the work. However it must be pointed out that one cannot make a silk purse out of a sow's ear, and planetary hours are limited in their effect unless fortified by planetary influences so therefore cannot be expected to produce results nearly as powerful as the Stellar powers.

Planetary hours are most useful for the making of inks, perfumes, minor magical implements and talismans of short duration and effect. An exception to this is when the Sun and Moon are conjunct in a sign that a planet rules, on its day and in its hour, and the planet itself is dignified by position and aspect and free from affliction.

The outer planets, Uranus, Neptune, and Pluto, are not generally used in Stellar Magick, as their influences are uncertain and often unfortunate and their invocation can be difficult. Uranus tends towards the sudden, unexpected, lightning-bolt type of activity;

Neptune has depths of secrecy which may be deceptive and even treacherous, and Pluto can be a tyrannical megalomaniac of transformation. In general however when a benefic configuration to be invoked is well aspected by Saturn, Uranus, Neptune or Pluto, the effect is not so much malefic as cohesive; the influence of the outer planets in Stellar Magick can be one of strengthening and activating the other planets. A minor bad aspect to one or more of them may serve to initiate events which may otherwise be balanced out of the equation by the general harmony, sweetness and light of the benefics; this kind of judgement requires some knowledge of astrological theory as well as practical experience of Stellar Magick. Nevertheless, bad aspects to the Moon should be avoided always.

THE SUN-VENUS

THERE IS ONE Solar aspect that stands alone in the reckoning of the Stellar Magickian, and that is the Sun's conjunction with Venus. Up to this point the Stellar Magickian has walked with his Gods in the knowledge that they will never desert him, for that is impossible. His consciousness will have been expanded by his experiences, but only as far as the boundaries of astrology allow, and so he has had no inkling of any sort of Dark Night of the Soul. That is a terrible experience, when the illumination that went before is withdrawn, the "God" is removed, and one is left alone and abandoned with feelings of intense desperation, aloneness, and emptiness. It is a further stage of Initiation, and the ritual of Sun conjunct Venus can be the start of a similar ordeal of fear and despair and division. Entering the Temple to honour the celestial Union of the God with the Goddess is not a step to be taken lightly. This initiation, known to us as the Ordeal X and described and explained in detail elsewhere, was discovered or re-discovered and researched by the O∴A∴A∴ in the late 1970s and early 1980s in the usual way, by hypothesis, experiment, catastrophe, and triumph.

Part of the research was published in *The New Equinox/British Journal of Magick* Volume 5 Part 3, after

Brother Leo (P-ACHAD-0) gave some of his notes to Ray Sherwin, the previous editor of the magazine, who used them in the article entitled "The Great Secret Revealed – and Concealed." Below is an excerpt from that essay.

"The time for commencing the initiatory process of Stellar magic is symbolised by the five pointed star. Anyone who has pondered over the sign of the pentagram in order to fathom its significance will have been totally dissatisfied by references to the Star of Bethlehem, the elements, microprosopus and so on, and rightly so. The pentagram, in its essential form, is not a manufactured symbol, a convenient unicursal glyph. It occurs naturally – in the heavens.

"In their conjunctions the Sun and Venus form a perfect pentagram every eight years, one point being made in approximately one year. It is as though these bodies are constantly inscribing the sign of the pentagram over the Earth – and the Sun and Venus are of supreme importance regarding the Key to Magic. This great secret has lain concealed over the centuries, from time to time it has almost percolated to the surface either through magical activity or, more recently, through publication.

"It is difficult to say with certainty that the Templars rediscovered it although this seems more than likely. Paracelsus knew the half of it for certain as did Eliphas Levi and both men came within a stroke of declaring its nature.

"For some reason the glory of the Key faded with the death of Levi; the leaders of the great magical revival were left groping in the dark. Blavatsky, Mathers,

Westcott and all the magicians and witches and warlocks and wizards who followed them were quite ignorant of the single fact which would have delivered them from their own confusion. Even Aleister Crowley, who came so close to it, merely skirted its periphery.

"To return for a moment to Eliphas Levi: in his 'Transcendental Magic' he makes the following statements about a particular sign:

"'The Quintessence itself is represented by (it)'

"'(it) is the sign of the word made flesh.'

"'This sign, ancient as history, and more ancient.'

"He goes on to say by what perfumes this sign should be consecrated. All are perfumes of an essentially female nature. Yet the sign to which he was referring was that of the pentagram.

"It is evident that Levi was not concerned with any common symbol scratched on stone or metal or the fetishes which festoon the gathered multitudes at occult tea-parties, since he goes on to mention the Morning Star and the Star of Lucifer, both being alternative names for the planet Venus; Venus, whose number, seven, occurs seven times on the Great Seal of the A∴A∴. In reference to the Heavenly or Blazing pentagram Eliphas Levi declared that its representation should be constructed of the seven metals on virgin white marble. Again we have an allusion to Venus, white marble being sacred to her and again we have the number seven in reference to the pentagram. This last point would seem to be an absurdity not only in the disparity of the numbers but also in the near impossibility of alloying the seven metals. So what did he mean? There has long been a tradition that Venus contains within herself a synthesis of the other planets. The Golden Dawn expressed this concept in its fifth knowledge lecture which contains a diagram of the ten sephiroth within the symbol of Venus.

"Only the diagram was given; its significance was not explained and another part of the Key was both revealed and concealed. By the word 'metal' Levi actually meant 'planet'. The synthesis of all the planets is expressed in Venus, and when the Sun forms a conjunction with her the Grand Elixir may be prepared.

"This is the time of The Great Initiation and if a ritual synchronised with this stellar configuration is performed by the candidate then all his experiences from that time until he is found worthy, will be initiatory.

"Even this initiatory process has been kept secret down the centuries, and has been veiled under many allegories, the most well known of which is the Twelve labours of Hercules. It causes the candidates to undergo an astrologically based process of change that continues with the Sun's passage through the Zodiac. It causes the candidates to be stripped of all they think about themselves and they are left with two ideas – who they are and who they are not – duality. This period can be from twelve months to a lifetime to never, depending upon the character of the candidate taking part in the initiation. How will he or she know when the initiation is complete? He will know! In this initiatory process the would-be Magician very soon realises that it is the Gods who are dealing with his soul and the changes he is going through are definitely 'Magical'. The candidate continues through his life as normal after the Rite but his experiences that have been provoked by his initiation will be anything but ordinary, he will literally experience the Twelve Labours of Hercules, and he will have to be truly Herculean if he is to win through these ordeals. The result of which will be in the first instance to unite the duality in his nature, the rest of the process cannot be the subject of this work and would require a separate treatise all of its own.

"It is not possible to illustrate what the ordeal will be for a given individual, as each will experience it in his or her own very personal way. The magic of the Stars is not to be undertaken lightly for once the initiatory process is undertaken it cannot be stopped, any more than the stars in their courses. Suffice to say a Stellar Magician is an individual to be respected, not simply for his power, but for his courage and humanity."

The practical work of performing the Sun conjunct Venus rituals did not involve any sex magick, regardless of the emphasis placed upon it in Sherwin's article. The O∴A∴A∴ instead constructed rituals of invocations to a High Priestess, who in her trance of possession by the Goddess, would prophesy, vivify elixirs and tinctures or consecrate talismans and weapons of appropriate attribution, and finally bless a cup of communion wine for the assembled ritualists.

The analysis by English Qaballistic methods of the symbols involved proved the theory of the Ordeal X. SUN+VENUS (36+71) = 107 = MAGICIAN, and SILENCE; while SUN AND VENUS (36+21+71) = 128 = BAPHOMET, SCARLET WOMAN, and THE ORDEAL X, indicating the uniting of the dualities in the candidate's psyche in the identification with these archetypes, and the qualities needed to accomplish such an integration. Over the next four or five years following the publication of the article quoted above the different stages of the Ordeal were identified and clearly defined. This also has been described elsewhere; here it will suffice to say that the candidate's journey is symbolised by the Zodiac Signs Libra, Scorpio, Sagittarius, and Capricorn, which have the sum total 418 (58+93+146+121). This number is of great significance in *Liber AL*, the source text of the English Qaballistic system, which calls the number "The Name of Thy House," in the penultimate verse of its Second Chapter. It is in this Initiatory sphere of Stellar Magick that the English Qaballa and the *Book of the Law* most closely inform the theory and practice of the Stellar Magickian, as the next section will demonstrate.

THE 418 QUATERNARY

THE SIGNS OF the Zodiac describe the continuous cycle of birth, life, death, afterlife, and rebirth, in which death is the crucial mystery. We will examine this cycle in the light of the English Qaballa's enumeration.

The body dies in the Sign of SCORPIO (=93=TIME, NATURE), the House of Death in astrological tradition; and the individual's consciousness enters the "Hades" condition where all the ideas the ego had about itself must be resolved: this happens in SAGITTARIUS (=146=HEREAFTER). When the ideas about oneself have been resolved one is free to enter the "Paradise" state in CAPRICORN (=121=RAPTUROUS). The spirit then is poured from the paradise state to a lower vessel and is given another idea about itself in AQUARIUS the Water-Bearer (=95=THE STAR/CROSS/BLOOD). This idea begins to concrete into form in PISCES (=97=ITSELF) where as a child or seed it enters the world at ARIES (=66=BABE, EARTH), the First House in an astrological chart and the Sign of the Vernal Equinox. As the seed-idea-child goes beneath the horizon it forgets all that has gone before, and begins to acquire independent characteristics in TAURUS (=76=THING), which rules the Second

House, representative of the individual's possessions. In the Third House, signifying communication, the separate ego develops and notions of "self" and "not-self" arise – the Twins of GEMINI (=117=THE TWIN, LETTERS). In the Fourth House which is the home and the mother, ruled by CANCER (=78=NUIT, TEST), this new ego is tested in young adulthood by the Goddesses manifested on the Earth. From this inter-reaction a mature adult is born that is a concrete representation of its terrestrial experience up to that point, in LEO (=34=FOOL) the Fifth House ruling all matters of fun and pleasure and romance. This adult-ego is then examined in the House of health – the Sixth which is ascribed to VIRGO (=63=BIND) – by illness. LIBRA (=58=ORDEALS) is the point of balance with and against Aries, it is the place of judgement, and anything which does not balance becomes the cause of death in SCORPIO – and furthermore is transferred as Karma to the future point of terrestrial birth in Aries. It will be noted that all signs-houses-states are tested and balanced by their opposite. Furthermore, the Zodiac is a fluid flowing circle with no end nor beginning, and all signs affect each other, they cannot be considered in total isolation.

In this sequence the mysterious and therefore interesting bit is the passage between Libra, the Balance between Life and Death; through Scorpio and Sagittarius, to Capricorn, the state of being in Paradise. This is what is referred to in AL II:78, "the Name of Thy House 418" since as we have said these four Signs have the value 418 by E.Q. We cannot enlarge upon this subject here but we must emphasise that the period when the Moon is in Scorpio is a particularly unsafe and unfortunate time. The performance of Stellar Magick while the Moon is in the House of Death is not recommended: in fact we heartily advise the student to forget it. Astrologers will know that Horary or Electional charts should be discarded if the Moon be found in the Via Combusta or Burning Way which extends from 15 degrees Libra to 15 degrees Scorpio. Events are dangerously unpredictable at this time. In our experience the period of uncertainty continues until the Moon leaves Scorpio.

One young probationer was not convinced by what he was told about Moon in Scorpio. He arranged a day trip for himself and a friend who was an Adept of the O∴A∴A∴ with several years experience of Stellar Magick and the effects of the Moon in Scorpio. Unsurprisingly, he demurred somewhat when the Probationer rang him up to tell him about his plan. "Oh," quoth the Probationer, "don't worry about that. I'm bigger than Scorpio." "Not on my phone, you're not," replied the Adept, nearly dropping the instrument in shock at his friend's untimely arrogance. "She will have Her way with us, you'll see." On the day appointed they got into their car and set off, and had hardly turned the corner when they were pulled over by a policeman. Our Probationer ruefully handed over his driving licence while the Adept just smiled quietly. It turned out that the policeman was known to the Probationer who had had some unpleasantness with him a number of years ago. The policeman was off duty and in a really bad mood, clearly bent on giving someone else a hard time to alleviate his own misery. The two friends managed to talk him down, and eventually got under way again, with exhalations and raised eyebrows. A few hundred yards further on they encountered a small but intense riot, at which point they gave up and went home, and the chastened Probationer began to revise his opinion of Scorpio.

Another interesting example lies in the negotiations leading up to the hand-over of Hong Kong by the British to China. A series of meetings and indeed the final ceremony were all held with the Moon in Scorpio, and the general opinion was that Hong Kong was doomed to a bleak future under Chinese rule. Nobody guessed that capitalism would spread to the mainland instead and catapult China's population into the 21st Century.

We can see from these and many more examples that the Zodiac acts rather like a filing system which is accessed on a day to day basis by the Moon. Each sign is a file of information consistent with the sign. As the Moon progresses through a sign the individual is impressed with the same information and ideas from the file, which has been updated by his experience at the last transit through the sign. The Moon governs the unconscious and the unconscious governs the personality: the actions, principles, and motives of the personality are all generated by the unconscious Moon. Thus when the Moon is in Scorpio everything existent during that time will die or at least will not relate to the past and future, but remain isolated in a capsule of non-expressability. One tends to think of the same things over and over again month in month out for years but nothing comes of them; plans are made in Scorpio but they lead a perverse life or have no life at all, anything but follow the original ideas of the planner.

The Stellar magickian approaches the collective filing system (unconscious, Astral plane or whatever one likes to call it) and modifies it according to his will using symbol systems appropriate to the requirements of the Sign. In practice the principle is more complex than this as it is rarely possible to affect the Astral filing system from below and the magickian usually waits until there is a potent astrological configuration.

A SHORT STUDY OF PLUTO IN 418

PLUTO MOVES SO slowly that his characteristics as they are modified by each successive Zodiac Sign affect a whole generation of humanity. In one Sign he sees the children born who will share the experiences of transformation characterised by the next Sign. When Pluto was in Leo and World War 2 was happening, for example, the children were born who would shape the cultural changes of the 1960s. The Virgo generation who grew up in the 1970s politely distanced themselves from their parent's excesses and invented punk rock, and set about remaking the world. They were a hard working studious generation who became analysts of everything from financial markets to high grade weapons and pharmaceuticals, and signals from outer space. Their hedonistic Pluto/Leo parents continued to enjoy themselves as much as possible, perhaps somewhat bemused by their unadventurous offspring, who in turn probably found the behaviour of their elders a little lacking in gravitas. Then came the 1980s, and nothing would ever be the same again.

Since the first observations of Pluto in the modern age occurred the force of his influence has become more and more noticeable, and so we knew that his journey through 418 should produce some remarkable changes. In fact the adolescent Pluto-Virgo/Libra generation witnessed the judgement, execution, and hasty burial of all manner of sacred cows in the years that Pluto was in the House of Death; some of which had been cherished for centuries, others younger and less beloved but still seemingly immovable. There was the collapse of Communism and the lifting of the Cold War's curse of threatened nuclear annihilation. There were all kinds of civil unrest, and social and economic upheavals on a previously unimaginable global scale. The computer age leapt forward from the inventiveness of the Sixties generation, and the influence of Pluto in Libra which had done its best to make peace not war decided to make profit instead, and balanced its accounts accordingly.

1984 was the year that Pluto properly entered Scorpio. There was a story at the time that the number 1984 when pushed through a Hebrew Kabbalistic wringer came out with the words "God is Dead" and certainly there was a distinct weakening and diluting of the credibility of establishment Christianity both Catholic and Protestant, while Islam responded to the perceived danger in the only way it knew, by direct action; but that was the tip of the fatal iceberg that was destined to collide with the fabric of society. As Pluto gained strength in Scorpio there came the AIDS epidemic, and the nuclear disaster at Chernobyl; there were threats of alien invasion, and rumours of government conspiracies and cover-ups; and Capitalism began to show its ugliest face as market forces became the guiding light of international policy-makers. Oddly enough, the manuscript of *Liber AL*, lost since the death of Karl Germer, was found in an attic in Berkeley, California, in 1984.

It was around this time that we began to take proper notice of Pluto and what he was doing. Our understanding of 418 led us to believe that it should be a lifetime period of major social transformation, with four distinct phases. We found that his orbit takes about 248 years and back-projecting Pluto in 418 we found that last time around was the Age of Enlightenment; and going back into history we discovered that the decades around 33AD were also part of a Pluto 418 period. We were not completely surprised, therefore, when Pluto in Sagittarius saw the whole world connected together and talking to itself via the internet, long-distance travel both physical and metaphorical becoming popular, and the traditions, philosophies, and religions of the world's accumulated wisdom suddenly accessible for all who were interested in such matters to expand their knowledge. Meanwhile the children of the Pluto/Scorpio era went off to fight a catastrophically murderous campaign in the Middle East, which, having started with the Moon in Scorpio, has dragged on into the Pluto/Capricorn period and is obscuring the spiritual transformation that is also taking place.

Having learned to recognise the stages of 418 we were able to make some predictions about the first decades of the 21st century, based on our knowledge of local conditions, and the fact that while Uranus was in Aries (ruling England, Japan, and Syria) he was in square aspect to Pluto. One interpretation of that configuration was that all things ruled by Aries would feel that transforming influence most strongly. In 2011 Brother Leo accurately predicted the riots in England's major cities some months in advance, and the manner in which they would be resolved. He also made some more general predictions concerning the ruthless exposure of corruption in society and uncovering of lies which had been festering for half a century or more. These predictions were published on the internet for a short space of time. Anyone can project the characteristics of the Pluto/Capricorn generation onto the qualities of Aquarius when expressed as the Power of Transformation, and draw their own conclusions; but who would have said at the end of the last time Pluto made the Pilgrimage through 418, as Wedgwood was putting together his pottery business and Arkwright's mills were gently chugging away in Lancashire, that within a lifetime England's canal system would have come and gone to leave the countryside traversed by railways, or that the French King would be dead, or that America would have declared Independence, or half a dozen other momentous changes would occur whose seeds had germinated and begun to grow during the Age of Enlightenment? We may be in for a bumpy ride!

ALCHEMY

THE METHODS OF Alchemy have always been hedged about with secrecy. The substances prepared by this Art confer such great power that the secrets of their preparation must remain guarded, lest the profane in surprising its mystery cause great harm by their ill-considered experiments.

There is no short cut to the completion of the Great Work; nevertheless it is considered by many to be the Crown of Magic, so we have included the method of its working. We have not broken with tradition, and we too have veiled the mystery of this Art in allegory and symbolism. To perform this Art the magician must be initiated into all forms of magic. The more he knows, the greater are his arms in combatting the snares and pitfalls of this great Art.

The cycle of the Sun is from Scorpio to Scorpio, but there is death in Scorpio. Its death must always be under good stars, so that its conception is under good stars. If it dies in Scorpio then the chain is broken. The original material must be heated again and again, but only when the stars are helpful, or the delivery of its nature will be affected.

This aspect has been totally neglected by modern would-be Alchemists. The power of the first matter is improved by constant reheating. Only when the luminosity of the first matter reaches incandescence is it ready to be distilled over into the Circubit, but it must be delayed until Jupiter or Venus are elevated. The stars at the time of distillation must reflect the requirements of the Alchemist.

It is always wisest to reflux until all impurity in the prima materia has been removed. Each time it is reheated the Gods must be invoked to assist. The prima materia must be put in the vessel under the finest stars possible.

The process is begun by gently heating with the Philosopher's fire that must not burn the hands, so that the light in the Temple of the Sun is constant. Do not attempt to do more than this. This heating should be gentle without the reflux condenser. Repeat the gentle heat four times for Jupiter and seven times for Venus. The prima materia should have mixed sufficiently by this time, and will now be ready to be converted into the Philosopher's mercury. The Moon would ideally be applying to a conjunction with Jupiter or Venus during this operation.

Reflux until all the original material reaches a steady incandescence; this should take between 10 and 100 refluxings. It is easy to tell when the conversion to mercury is achieved, as upon testing a small drop it will enable the Alchemist to enter the Astral plane and confer with the spirits.

At this point great care will be needed as the powers of the Philosopher's mercury can be so great as to destroy the vessel in which it is contained. Only a very gentle refluxing is demanded now, always taking care that the Moon is free from affliction and moving to good aspects. The distillation must be performed under the finest stars possible: it must always be remembered that the end of any operation is the beginning of another.

The distillation must be as gentle as possible so as not to get any dross in the Circubit. Heat very gently until the Elixir just begins to come over, then stop the heat until boiling ceases. Begin again, all the while invoking the Deities to thy aid. When all the Elixir has been distilled over, allow it to cool and place it in a well stoppered bottle that has been consecrated to the Gods who preside over the spirit contained.

Some considerable practice is needed in the Art of Alchemy. Do not expect to succeed without having become adept in all the stages; for although there is great power in the Art, each stage needs the utmost delicacy.

It is wise to begin by experimenting with each stage of the operation until by diligence it is perfected. Start by heating gently and noting the changes that take place with each stage of the operation, so that nothing is a surprise to one.

The Circubit must be of the finest glass, without flaw, for on its disposition depends the whole operation. It should have a water jacket; the water must not be cold, but of a gentle warmth. The control of the temperature is critical during the final distillation, as if it is too cold the material will not distil correctly, and if the water is too hot vapour will escape from the receiving vessel and an explosion will be the likely result.

THE PART OF FORTUNE

I WISH NOW to consider an astrological phenomenon vital to the practice of Stellar Magick which is neither planetary nor Zodiacal but a condition in space. It at first appears to be one of those bits of Astrological impedimenta that has come down to us from the mists of antiquity with seemingly little purpose or meaning, and yet as is often the case with occult symbols, the apparently unimportant conceals a great mystery. This was never more true than with the Pars Fortuna, or Part of Fortune.

It is a factor in astrological work that has been neglected by modern astrologers as its function is not obvious in Natal Astrology. Its symbol is a cross in a circle, and it is a magical concept and belongs in ritual Astrology. Indeed it is one of the most important factors in Stellar Magick.

The position of the Part of Fortune is generated by adding the longitude of the Ascendant to the longitude of the Moon and subtracting the longitude of the Sun. In Mundane Astrology the formula varies according to whether it is day or night; for the Stellar Magickian however the same formula applies throughout. To understand how this equation works to produce an imaginary point that holds the key to wealth and fortune we must examine what we are actually doing when we subtract the Sun from the Ascendant combined with the Moon.

The Ascendant is the ego, it is the part of the chart that reveals itself to the world. The Moon is the personality derived from unconscious sources that reflect the light of individuality, which is the Sun. These three symbols, Sun, Moon, and Ascendant, combine to give an ego that is unconsciously directed. To remove the power of the Sun from this entity would render it an empty container. Without the Sun, the Ascendant and Moon combined become an empty vessel, without power and energy. They become unfulfilled desire, a concept not met with in the planetary scheme.

This symbol appears banal and unimportant and yet it is one of the most potent symbols in the whole mystery of Magic. The circle crossed represents a container so negative that it would almost be a black hole in space, consuming all that came near it and changing its plane of existence from the macro-cosmic plane of the stars to the microcosmic plane of the world, and individual existence. Fortuna is the cup ready to be filled, the waiting earth, the receptacle of the power of the stars: a supreme negativity that could only be described in ideographic terms as a Goddess. This is She who takes all from the Stars and gives all to the world, She who devours the blood of the Stars for all eternity; this is the ancient lost Goddess who gives all. Her symbol, the cross of harmony within the circle of the essence of woman's femininity, is to be found in many symbols almost concealed. It is the final perfection of the symbol of Venus which is a cross surmounted by a circle, where the cross at last harmonises the circle. It is the symbol of the Earth, the unfertilised seed that is the living Goddess who by Her power gives at all times, wherever She is found.

The symbol and its ramifications would be more aptly named Isis. The genesis of the Goddess Isis was already unknown to the Egyptians who worshipped her. Her origins go back beyond the bounds of prehistory; yet her nature is essentially the same as that of the Part of Fortune. Fortuna, the Moon personified with the addition of the Ascendant, is Isis going on her search around the Zodiac for the dismembered body of Osiris and finally seeking the Solar phallus. Isis is the great mother, the ultimate mother; and just as the terrestrial mother takes the power from her man and uses that power to feed her children, so Isis-Fortuna takes the power of the stars and gives it to the earth; the great winged disk of the Goddess traverses eternity, drinking the blood of the Stars to feed the children of Earth. She has been mistaken as a Solar emblem, because She is the woman who is "clothed with the Sun" but He is not inside Her and can only radiate His power upon Her. She can contain the power of the Sun but as a cup: He can never be truly within Her.

This Goddess has been in exile for many thousands of years. An exile that has been caused in part by the inability of Adepts to place her astronomically. Her characteristics cannot be found among the natures of the female planets Venus, Saturn, the Moon or even the Earth; although the Earth most nearly encompasses her nature, that is why they both share the same symbol. The Earth feeds her Children in the same way our Part of Fortune or Isis feeds the Earth, but the Earth is the secondary source of sustenance: always the primary source is Isis. The Goddess who has been lost for thousands of years can now be reinstated as the great benefic, greater even than Jupiter because Isis-Fortuna gives the benefits from whatever she touches. She is the only astrological phenomenon that cannot afflict. It is hardly surprising that she was considered supreme by all the great Stellar civilisations who worshipped her, and continued to worship her even though her source had been lost.

The Part of Fortune is a Cup into which 'the streams of blessing' are poured by the planets. The symbol is found in the Ace of Cups by Pamela Coleman Smith in A. E. Waite's Tarot, where it is held suspended over the Cup by a Dove. This symbolism is resumed in the Glyph of the O.T.O.

The symbolism of the Ace of Cups gives the formula completely. When Venus (the Dove) is conjunct Pars Fortuna it pours blessing into the emotional nature (water). It is thus an Astronomical symbol of The Holy Grail that represents the nature of the Grail in man at any given time. The empty container that is Ascendant + Moon – Sun represents the state of man's soul when it is unenlightened. It is this state of unenlightenment which makes it a vehicle for any force it meets in its search for energy. It is a symbol of earth which takes up all the forces that are directed to it by the cosmos, without discrimination. The Grail or Part of Fortune itself transmutes the power: as the earth transmutes the power of the cosmos into energies to sustain itself, so Fortuna takes the energies from the cosmos to sustain the individual. On a lower level it takes material wealth – the Part of Fortune indicates where this is in a chart – on a higher level as the Grail it takes spiritual energy.

As material wealth should be used to worship the Gods (as in the prehistoric Stellar civilisations), so spiritual "wealth" or energy should sustain the individual Soul and bring it to its essential nature, that of the Gods. It is the removal of the Solar Power that is the Key to its mystery. The Grail is darkened by the loss of the Sun, just as the Soul is darkened by its loss of the Spiritual light. There is a choice: it can choose.

Humanity feels this loss of Spirit, and feels a sense of inadequacy and emptiness as a consequence: but most often seeks the easy way out and comforts itself with the pale reflection of Spiritual wealth – material wealth. Of course when material wealth is gained it sustains the body; but the Soul is still empty, and unsatisfied, and the search goes on – maybe over several incarnations – until the Soul realises its true destiny and begins the Quest for what it already has – the Holy Grail. The postulant goes on the search for the Grail, but in fact the search is for the spiritual light of the Sun that illuminates the Grail, so that he can at last see it for what it is.

The Holy Grail is the desire nature in man. It is never fulfilled by material gain, no matter how great that gain is. The desire nature is represented in the chart by the Pars Fortuna, that imaginary point at which spiritual wealth will pour into the individual's life. It is not a physical reality just as the Part of Fortune is not a physical reality.

The connection with Jupiter and the Wheel of Fortune is resumed in the idea of wealth and prosperity. Both ideas of a Grail Cup and a Wheel contain the same symbol – they are female sexual symbols. As the female must be filled with light or life so the Grail must be filled with light and the Part of Fortune fulfilled by the power it meets. All these symbols vibrate with the same power in different forms: life, material wealth, spirituality, and the Sun, all represent the same energy on different levels.

That aspect of Stellar lore that was once called the Grail is now simply the Part of Fortune. That which once contained the light, is now merely the container of material wealth, but the symbol has always remained the same, as a beacon to the wise, and an illusion to the ignorant. Just as the great Lord Jupiter begins by giving a feeling of happiness and ends by showing you he is the image of the great beneficent God, so the Part of Fortune begins by showing where wealth is to be found and ends by revealing the Container of the Spiritual Truth, the inheritor of Karma and the secret of the universe – The Holy Grail.

The Part of Fortune conjuncts all the planets every day. The Stellar magickian who invokes Venus-Fortuna conjunctions EACH day for, say, one lunar month, with a simple ritual of invocation involving the burning of suitable incense, will find that it is not a chore, as these divinities, once contacted, act directly and beneficially on the consciousness. The continuous invocation of Venus maintains the magician in contact with the Love of the Universe, and this love will pervade all his experience. It is not really possible to explain the effect of the shift in consciousness that the invocation and worship of these deities bring. There is no need for faith, there is a knock at the door and the stellar powers always answer.

One O∴A∴A∴ member wrote, "My own experience was an almost helter skelter shift in orientation from the hum drum to the sublime in a very short time. Everything starts to "go right". Life becomes delightful as the events in one's life become influenced by the good offices of "The Gods". Everything runs smoothly. The harmony with the universe provokes harmony from the world. For the first time one is living in Harmony with the Cosmos. There is very much a feeling of "The battle is over" as the world begins to be on your side, instead of fighting you every step of the way. You have allied yourself with The Powers that control the Earth. The PERPETUAL sense of conflict disappears. A new consciousness dawns, like awakening from sleep to a beautiful day, but the day can last for the rest of your life and become more beautiful and real as your participation with the LIVING cosmos grows."

The observation was made that the Fortuna rites can also be used to raise the spirits of others:

"My mother who is given to the glooms of old age and her Sun in Capricorn has been greatly uplifted by the spirits of Jupiter after I requested that Jupiter turn his influence to the impossible task of dispelling her Capricornian glooms. Despite her failing eyesight she cheered up and returned to her hobby of knitting, abandoned for several years, and renewed her interest in the garden and flowers to the extent that our house looked more like a florist's shop.

"By far the most interesting phenomena associated with Fortuna is the immediate closeness and communion with the Gods and Goddesses. One finds an initial disbelief of the results that one receives only to have one's doubts dispelled in a very real and personal way. By invoking the virtues of the Goddesses and Gods and their wisdom, universal truths are irrefutably brought into one's daily consciousness. The only requirement being knowing of the time of Fortuna and above all a pure heart."

Each day at dawn the Moon is conjunct Isis-Fortuna. This means that at dawn the personality (which is ruled by the Moon) is a chalice for the stellar influences. This explains the strange feeling of oneness with the universe that is experienced by mystics and others at this time, and is the reason for the emphasis on performing their invocations then. The personality is flooded with the Divine Will at dawn and this is felt by anyone who can stand still and open their awareness at that time. It is the time of The Grail, and the spiritual man who worships at dawn will find his cup of spirituality filled. Even the most ignorant of men cannot fail to be moved by the Dawn, even his soul will be stirred by the rising Sun, even the grail in his empty heart is briefly illuminated as the emptiness of the celestial Grail is temporarily filled by the light, but then unlike the spiritual Sun, the temporal Sun moves on and the magic moment of the Grail is lost and the man moves on, conscious that he has seen something beautiful, but unable to really say what it was. The mystery is that he has had a fleeting glimpse of the Grail.

HOW BROTHER LEO CAME TO WRITE
THE STELLAR RITUALS

OUR RESEARCHES INTO the significance and magickal use of the Part of Fortune began in the mid 1980s at the beginning of the home computer age, when the BBC computer with its 5.25 inch floppy disk drive was the popular choice. Leo had an early but adequate astrology program which allowed the user to produce print-outs of natal and progressed charts and the current transits of planets and other points, including the Part of Fortune. Synchronistically there came into our midst one Trevor Langford, Brother Daedalus, who was a programming genius bursting with enthusiasm as only a young man with the Sun in Aries can be. Daedalus succeeded in altering the astrology program so that it would calculate and print the times of every planetary Fortuna conjunction for every day, for a period of one month.

The symbol of the Part of Fortune, ⊕, seemed highly significant in itself, and not just because it appears in the manuscript of *Liber AL* with the words "this circle squared in its failure is a key" on the well-known Sheet 16 of AL III:47. Our theoretical research, outlined above, led us to seriously consider the possibilities of rituals timed to synchronise with this phenomenon, especially when we realised that dawn could present several features of interest all at once. The Moon in favourable aspect to Venus or Jupiter and going conjunct Fortuna, for example, seemed too good to miss. Fortuna moves quickly around the Zodiac and Her conjunctions last about eight minutes, making the ritual moment ideal for fast operations such as drawing a sigil, blessing a talisman, or creating a tincture. We experienced a little set-back when someone pointed out that FORTUNA=93, and indeed She does have a wry sense of humour, as this early record shows:

"The time of my daily ritual of Fortuna conjunct Venus approached. I prepared by having a bath. Climbing out of my bath I clothed myself in my new emerald green bath towel and stood before my altar.

"'O Venus Goddess of love and art. I adore thee, goddess of nature, bless my phallus with thy love and force so that my love be ever dedicated to thee. Come swiftly and without delay through Fortuna, and fill my life with thy joy and laughter.

"'I burn thy incense, I light the flame in thy lamp in the grace and love of the beautiful star... So mote it be, Amen.'

"So concluded my brief invocation. I left my altar and went to dress myself. I collapsed in laughter for Venus had indeed blessed my phallus, for the green dye of my new towel had run colouring my member a beautiful shade of emerald. Never doubt the humour of the Gods for they touch your heart.

"I mused – was it possible for the Gods to improve one's finances by bestowing money directly asked for upon one's person? I chose a Fortuna conjunct Jupiter and performed the appropriate rite. I included the words 'send thy angels o Jupiter to bestow upon me money without delay.'

"Twenty-four hours later I had cause to go to the bank where much to my amusement all the staff of the bank were in fancy dress as angels. I was handed my money by a cashier-Angel complete with wings and halo."

After much discussion and number crunching we found the name Isis-Fortuna to be satisfactory, and that was the name of the spirit we would invoke at dawn. (ISIS-FORTUNA=56+93 = 149 = JESUS CHRIST=68+81). There were at least half a dozen members who were desirous of working Isis-Fortuna rituals on a regular basis, and that presented a difficulty, for it was not possible to convene the group with such frequency. Yet for research purposes it was necessary that everyone performed more or less the same ritual. So one afternoon Leo sat down with pen and paper and the good graces of an astro-qaballistic muse, and wrote the rituals which are presented later on in this book. At this time the group had expanded and consequently there was a wide variety of experience and knowledge among the membership; accordingly the rituals are short and simple, following a traditional pattern with invoking hexagrams and Names from the Sepher Yetzirah, and constructed along lines which would not be unfamiliar to anyone with even a slight acquaintance with traditional Western Occultism. Nonetheless, they work, just as they are, and they are adaptable too, once some understanding of the Stellar powers has been attained.

In the intervening years the so-called Abrahamic God-Names and Orders of Archangels and Angels seem to have fallen out of favour somewhat among occultists; and yet these appellations are as familiar as the Latin planetary names, or the stars named in Greek or Arabic, and they are easily apprehended by the higher levels of consciousness because of the life and strength they have gathered from centuries of continuous use. Since this particular system of Stellar Magick is underpinned by the English Qaballa on the Foundation of the *Book of the Law*, we accord all due respect and admiration to the JEWS=49=CROWN, KEY, and MOON, for they "have the half," as *Liber AL* states in verse 47 of the first Chapter. It is, after all, the sounds of these Names that is important, not the Kabbalistic secrets of the Hebrew language. One of the great achievements of the 20th Century Occult Revival was the indubitable demonstration that the correspondences of the old Tree of Life are applicable to systems beyond the realm of the Hebrew Kabbalistic Alphabet.

2. PREPARATION

How to time a Stellar Rite, cardinal correspondences, planetary correspondences, planetary feasts, the weapons of Stellar Magick, planetary talismans, basic ritual housekeeping and Temple etiquette.

HOW TO TIME A STELLAR RITE

A CURRENT EPHEMERIS and the ability to read it are indispensable for a ritualist wishing to synchronise his magickal work with the Stars, for he can rapidly scan the planetary positions and configurations to find something suitable, and only requires the additional knowledge of the time difference between that given in the ephemeris and his own time zone to fix the dates and times at which his Magickal Will will be best served by such an operation. There are so many variables involved that it can be months before a chart emerges that is anything like ideal, but those times are well worth waiting for.

Let us suppose, then, that we have discovered a Venus trine Jupiter occurring in the near future. We will check the positions of the two Deities on the day in question. Are they sufficiently established in the Sign – do they have more than 3 and less than 27 degrees? If not, then their influences will be somewhat diminished. Do they have any dignity in the Signs in which we find them? If not, then again the effect of the ritual will be slightly lessened; but we will assume that they are well dignified in Fire Signs, Jupiter in Sagittarius, which he rules, and Venus in Leo, whose passionate and romantic nature suits the Goddess very nicely. If either is within

3 degrees of harmonious aspect to their position in our Natal chart we may expect a heightened empathy with the spirits belonging to that Deity in our invocations.

Then we must examine the activity of the Moon. We are looking for a favourable lunar aspect, preferably a conjunction, while the planetary aspect is applying. The planetary aspect must be applying by at least 6 degrees; any further apart and they would be "out of orb" and too distant to have any effect on each other, and if they have begun to separate then whatever forces are invoked can only rapidly dissipate as well. The lunar conjunction with Jupiter in Sagittarius is less desirable since the Moon will be traversing 418 and for two or three days before the proposed ritual she will be very unfortunately placed, and most likely to bring disruption to any plans or arrangements made during that time. (It should also be remembered that Stellar rituals are less likely to work with the Moon in Capricorn, for there she is at her weakest and has little or no power to reflect the celestial influences.) It might be possible to squeeze in with the Moon in Libra where she would sextile both Venus and Jupiter but only if they are all at less than 15 degrees, leaving a decent margin before the Moon gets into the Burning Way, but that too is somewhat inadvisable. The Moon in Aries would form a trine with Venus and Jupiter, and complete the configuration known to astrologers as a Grand Trine, with all points of the triangle occupied. Aries would bring extra impetus to the Moon's reflection of the harmony between Venus and Jupiter, and it should be a nice ritual, with a suggestion of warm springtime, and of the King and Queen of Faerie – a good time to plant a seed. A lunar conjunction with Venus would be the most satisfactory configuration for a ritual, for from there the Moon would directly transmit the beauty and all-inspiring love of Venus, majestically enthroned in the Sign of the Lion and made perfect by the harmony with Jupiter, the beneficent King.

So far, then, in this idealised example, we have a Venus trine Jupiter, with the Moon going conjunct Venus before the trine occurs. Now we must have a look at what else the Moon gets up to before she leaves the Zodiac Sign, and in particular take note of what the last aspect is. This is important, for the lunar aspects that occur between our planetary configuration and the end of the Sign tell the story of the result of marking the moment, and the final aspect will colour the outcome of the ritual. Malefic final aspects should be examined most carefully, and of course the wisest course of action is to abandon the whole idea, especially in the event of something like Moon conjunct Saturn, or square Mars, or opposite Neptune, to name three of the worst. As we have said, Saturn causes a slowing down of affairs at best, and restrictions, which may be due to illness. Mars will bestow energy at any opportunity, but can lead to rash behaviour, accidents, and fires. Uranus is similar but with an explosive surprise element, and Neptune often takes something away and may bring deceptions, poisonings, and secret enemies, or trouble connected with the sea. Pluto, the planet of Transformation and also in charge of large organisations is hard to predict, but is not likely to bring good news when in square, opposition, or conjunction with the Moon.

By now our investigations with the ephemeris should ideally have yielded a nice planetary aspect applying, with a nice lunar aspect, and no trouble afterwards. These are the most important conditions for a successful ritual of Stellar Magick. Once these details have been checked and found adequate we can proceed to work out other finer details of timing; if any of these conditions are found wanting however, we can only say that we probably would not risk the consequences of marking such an event.

It is wise to draw the chart or get it up on screen at this point, for now we want to look at the House positions. Since the Moon takes roughly 2.2 hours to move one degree and we allow up to six degrees of orb applying to an aspect, we have a period of 12 hours or so in which to find a suitable time for our ritual. We use our chart to tweak the timing with the technique known to Horary Astrologers as "tilting" which is simply a matter of rotating the chart. The Houses remain fixed around the circle of the chart, which represents the whole sky, while the wheel of the Zodiac turns anti-clockwise within it. The Sun, Moon, and planets climb the eastern sky to the midheaven and so on round to set in the west. (See diagram at the end of this section.) One can tell the time of day represented in a chart by noting the position of the Sun – a handy trick if one is not sure of one's calculations! – but computers make light work of these technicalities, and even a very basic program will be able to draw a chart for a particular time, date, and location, in a matter of seconds. Therefore, if we want to perform our ritual at dawn, we will turn the chart until the Sun is on the Ascendant or just below, in the First House. Very often it is the case that one planet has far more dignity than the other, and we may want to bring it to the fore by placing it in the Tenth, so we turn the chart accordingly, and look at where that has put everyone else. When the second planet is in trine, it will end up in the Second House (property) or the 6th (health, and also servants and inferiors). Under these circumstances a significant talisman could be made the dwelling of a significant spirit. A ritual for a new beginning would be served by one of our planets in the First House which is the House of inception, birth, initiation, and so forth.

We also must remember to keep an eye on where the rest of the Gods and Goddesses are. We do not want any nasty surprises in the Seventh House, which is where we find whatever is facing us in partnership or in opposition. As usual, Saturn and Mars are the worst culprits, and should be somewhere else if possible. Saturn is quite happy in the Twelfth House, Mars is safe enough in the Third or the Ninth. Planets in retrograde motion do not seem to quite know what they are doing and can be rather vague and muddled in their effect, and sometimes when they go direct there comes another echo of the ritual, especially if the stellar configuration then occurs a second time. The same sorts of qualities have been noticed with planets which are intercepted at the chosen time and thus not quite in the same realm as the rest of the chart.

The following account furnishes an excellent example of the importance of accurate timing, and also highlights the synchronicities between the performance of Stellar Magick and the bigger picture of the magickian's life as delineated by his astrology, which occasionally force his hand into a course of action which is apparently quite stupid.

An alchemist of our acquaintance found a Venus sextile Jupiter well aspected by the Moon which seemed ideal for refining a particular tincture. He and his assistant performed the ritual, obtained their purified substance, and closed the proceedings with the customary feast. In pride of place on the table was the tincture in its consecrated bottle, surrounded with fresh roses. Suddenly the atmosphere changed from the regal joy and beauty which had prevailed from the invocations to the God and Goddess, becoming all at once dark and sinister. Petals had fallen from the roses, and there came wriggling out from amongst the blooms a mass of little green caterpillars. The two magickians hurriedly closed the ritual and cleared away their unwelcome visitors, and put the unfortunate tincture at the back of a locked cupboard. When the alchemist checked his ephemeris and charts again he found that the last aspect of the Moon before she left the Sign was a square to Saturn.

While the bottle of tincture remained in the house, family bereavement and ill fortune and poor health continued to surround the lives of all who had been present at the ritual. The alchemist was obliged to devise a means for the safe disposal of the unlucky bottle and its contents. His assistant suggested the site of a pauper's graveyard known locally as Angel's Meadow, and on All Hallow's Eve they went there and finding an area that had been landscaped into a small garden with a dead tree on one side, they poured out the tincture over the tree's roots, and left the bottle at the entrance. A dense fog came down that night. A few days later they went back, and found the tree had been cut down, and rather mysteriously, four china cups had been left around the stump. The current of bad luck which had held them now let them go, and it was not until the following Spring that the subject came up again, and the magickians returned to Angel's Meadow.

They found that synchronicity still prevailed, with an up-coming festival called "Not Quite Light" featuring a dawn event entitled "Breakfast With The Dead" in the Angel's Meadow itself, organized to raise money, food and clothing for the poor and destitute who in a different age would have been residents of that place. A photograph in the advertising showed the tree stump and two of the four cups; but the tree and its little garden where they had tipped the tincture away had vanished altogether, as if it were never there in the first place.

The alchemist later noted, "The moral of the story is, avoid rituals with bad aspects to Saturn! We certainly would have done if it hadn't have been invisible to us for some reason. The truth is that we were obviously meant to perform that rite in order to experience the already scripted ordeals that we were always destined to embark upon." It is this holistic awareness of the interconnectedness of all things which is integrated into the psyche of the Stellar Magickian and enables him to bear his ordeals with fortitude, giving him the grace and strength to help others who are suffering the same misfortune in a greater spiritual darkness. He will not waste time and energy looking for reasons why, but accepting the necessities of time's unfoldment and seeing the synchronicities of events, he will find the humility and sincerity in his heart to say "Not my will but Thine be done".

CARDINAL CORRESPONDENCES

THE FOLLOWING DIAGRAM is intended to help the beginner assimilate into his or her conscious mind some of the various attributes which are traditionally assigned to the four Quarters or compass points, North, East, South, and West. I have included the correspondences most useful to the Stellar Magickian: Archangelic Names, Elemental Weapons and colours; together with the Seasons and times of the day, and the Zodiac Sign and orientation of each Quarter. When we do not know where East is, we take it to be the direction in which we are facing, thus to make an Altar of an office desk we would place all the letter opening knives, scissors, and pencil sharpeners at the furthest side in front of us; all pens and pencils to the right, all pads of paper, mouse mats, paper weights and so forth on the left, and any sort of cup at the nearest edge. Communication devices probably would already be in front of us, in the East.

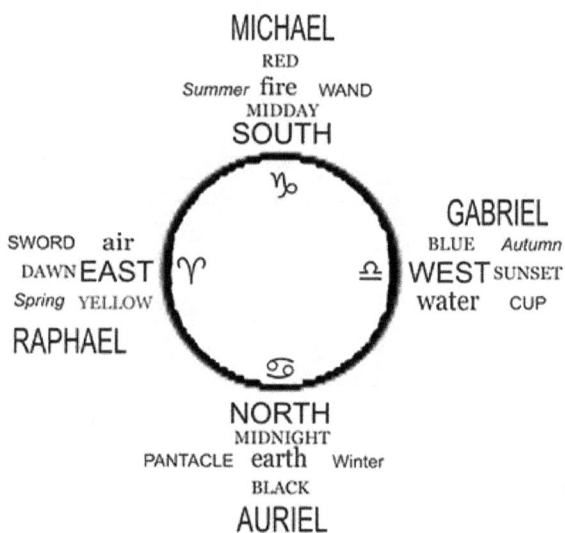

PLANETARY CORRESPONDENCES

HAVING OUTLINED THE various ritual techniques necessary for the successful practise of Stellar magic, we will now examine the individual attributes and correspondences for each planet in turn.

The experienced astrologer will note that many of the attributes discussed below are somewhat different to those normally applied with regard to natal and progressed astrology. These differences are easily explained by the change of standpoint from the more subjective fields of natal/progressed/mundane astrology to this highly objective field, which has more in common with horary and electional astrology.

The experienced occultist will note that many of the attributes discussed below are rather old-school traditional correspondences. This is not an argument that need detain us; the beginner will find that they work, and may gain the experience to add their own variations. We will merely point out that it is no longer necessary to visualise Hebrew letters for the successful vibration of God-Names, since the English Alphabet has been proven to be a Magickal Alphabet. We include the E. Qaballistic values for use in determining appropriate words and phrases for invocation.

THE SUN

⊙

Egyptian: OSIRIS, RA.	Greek: DIONYSOS, APOLLO.
Hebrew: JHVH ALOAH VE DAATH.	Archangel: RAPHAEL
Roman: APOLLO.	Nordic: BALDER.
Colour: CLEAR ROSE PINK.	Attribute: SOLAR PLEXUS.
Metal: GOLD.	Gemstones: DIAMOND.
Incense: OLIBANUM.	Plants: VINE.
Titles: BEAUTY.	Number: 6.
Symbols: LAMEN, ROSE CROSS.	E.Q. value: 36.

The Solar God is the Divine Priest-King of Heaven who rules but does not govern, the God who brings light and life to all. He is invoked for the harmony He brings as He confers the supreme authority upon the planets He aspects. His cycle through the Zodiac gives us the seasons and times of the year; although He appears to die and be reborn we know that His light is constant and undying: His power is of eternal life. He is the centre around which our universe exists.

The Solar God was known to the Greeks by many names – Apollo, the God of healing, Helios who drove the chariot of the Sun, and Dionysos who endured madness and suffering, and brought the gift of the vine to mankind. The Romans also named Him Apollo; the Egyptians named the Solar God according to His position in the sky, and worshipped Him as Ra, the Solar disk, and Osiris whose death and everlasting life was the inheritance they sought.

In our natal charts the Sun indicates the characteristics around which our personalities revolve. In ourselves He is represented by the solar plexus which is the centre of the body and the seat of intuition and Love; His symbols are the lamen which is worn upon the breast, and the Rose Cross which symbolises the spirit manifested upon the cross of the four elements. The colours of the Sun are rose-pink and yellow; the Solar metal is gold, and the diamond is His particular gemstone. Olibanum is the Solar incense, and the vine is the plant ruled by the Sun.

THE MOON

☽

Egyptian: SHU.	Greek: PERSEPHONE.
Hebrew: SHADDAI EL CHAI.	Archangel: GABRIEL.
Roman: DIANA.	Nordic: FRIGGA.
Colour: INDIGO.	Attribute: GENITALS.
Metal: SILVER.	Gemstones: MOONSTONE, PEARL.
Incense: JASMINE.	Plants: DAMIANA.
Titles: THE FOUNDATION.	Number: 9.
Symbols: THE PERFUMES AND SANDALS.	E.Q. value: 49.

The principle function of the Moon in Stellar Magick is to bring about a concrete manifestation of the effects of any given configuration. Thus, for feminine favours, one would celebrate a conjunction of the Moon and Venus. For wealth, the Moon and Jupiter.

The Moon is the Goddess of fertility and growth who reflects and embodies the rhythms of the Zodiac. Her cycles from new, waxing to full and waning to new – from the birth of growth in Aries to death and transformation in Scorpio and rebirth in Aries – are the key to all Nature's cycles; Her power is the flux and reflux of life, the Stellar Law of constant change. Hers is the nearest power to us in time and space – She is continually meeting and reflecting the influences of the Stars into every hour and day of our lives. Her power lies in the Astral plane, in whose light we see the hallucinatory images of the Gods. She is invoked in conjunction with the planetary deity (or deities) whose power we wish to be reflected into our lives to work therein the changes of our desire.

She has been called Persephone, whose sojourn in the Underworld gives fruitfulness to the Earth; the Egyptians named the lunar deity Shu, who exists between the earth and sky and supports the Heavens. The Romans worshipped the lunar Goddess in Her name of Diana.

In our natal charts She reveals the nature and force of our instinctive behaviour; in ourselves she is represented by the reproductive organs. Her symbols are the Perfumes and Sandals, which consecrate the Air as it nourishes the magician and the Earth that supports him in his work. Indigo and violet are the lunar colours; Her metal is silver, and the pearl and moonstone are Her gems. Jasmine is the incense of the Moon, and damiana is the plant ruled by Her.

MERCURY
☿

Egyptian: THOTH.	Greek: HERMES.
Hebrew: ELOHIM TZABAOTH.	Archangel: MICHAEL.
Roman: MERCURY.	Nordic: LOKI.
Colour: VIOLET PURPLE.	Attribute: LOINS & LEGS.
Metal: BRASS.	Gemstones: OPAL.
Incense: STORAX.	Plants: MOLY.
Titles: GLORY.	Number: 8.
Symbols: NAMES & VERSICLES.	E.Q. value: 115.

Mercury is the God of swiftness, acuteness and agility on all planes. His planet has the quickest orbit of the Sun, and He is always known as the Messenger of the Gods, whose inventiveness and magic is ever at the aid of mankind. His powers lie in the realms of thought and reason, and in the forms which embody the powers transcending them. The God Mercury is invoked conjunct the Moon when we desire swift articulate inspiration and mental agility to aid and control all Mercurial projects, and in conjunction with another planet He enhances the fulfillment of our wishes with acute clarity and rapidity.

By His Greek name of Hermes He is known as the God of trickery who invented the lyre and assisted Prometheus in obtaining for mankind a spark of the sacred fire of the Sun; He also helped the Heroes in their quests and ordeals. An aspect of Him was known to the Nordic races who called Him Loki. The Egyptians named Him the Lord of Wisdom and Magic, Thoth, who won five days of light from the Moon for the Birth of Osiris, Horus, Set, Isis, and Nepthys; the power of Mercury is always associated with invention and the Art and Science of Magic, and is always to the advantage of mankind.

In our natal charts Mercury influences our intellectual and reasoning intelligence, our ability to communicate, and reveals the nature of our mental interests and studies. In ourselves He is represented by the loins and legs, the part of the body whose muscular swiftness and strength supports and projects the magician in time and space. His symbols are the Names and Versicles – the words and Names of power. The colours of Mercury are violet-purple and orange; His metal is brass, and the opal is His gemstone. The incense is storax, and moly is the plant attributed to Mercury.

VENUS
♀

Egyptian: HATHOOR.	Greek: APHRODITE.
Hebrew: JHVH TZABAOTH.	Archangel: HANAEL.
Roman: VENUS.	Nordic: FREYA.
Colour: AMBER.	Attribute: LOINS, HIPS & LEGS.
Metal: COPPER.	Gemstones: EMERALD.
Incense: BENZOIN.	Plants: ROSE.
Titles: VICTORY.	Number: 7.
Symbols: LAMP & GIRDLE.	E.Q. value: 71.

Venus is the Goddess of Love. As we have noted, Her planet's conjunctions with the Sun form the heavenly pentagram which is the catalyst in the Stellar initiation of the magician; She is the Empress of the Stars, and Her Beauty is the beauty of the Stars. Her power lies in the mysteries of polarity and Love; She is the ever-virgin Goddess of space and nature. Her power is in all things of beauty and love and inspiration, in the Arts and all acts of creativity. She is invoked conjunct the Moon when we desire these blessings and the favours of Love, and when in conjunction with another planet She bestows Her gifts in union with the gifts of the deity invoked.

The Greeks knew Her by Her name Aphrodite, the Immortal who was born on the sea-foam and carried to shore in a mussel shell. Freya, the wife of Odin, She is named by the Norsemen. In Egypt She is named Hathoor, the patron Goddess of beautiful women and all artistic works. She is always associated with all that is best in women, and all artistic inspiration.

In our natal charts Venus reveals the nature and force of our closest relationships and love affairs, and influences our artistic and creative abilities. In ourselves She is represented by the loins, hips and legs, the part of the body which bears the reproductive organs but is not actually involved with the reproductive process – fertility is lunar, not Venusian. The symbols of Venus are the Lamp and the Girdle, and the Rose. Her colours are amber and emerald; Her metal is copper, and Her gemstone is the emerald. Her incense is benzoin, and the plant ruled by Her is the rose.

MARS
♂

Egyptian: HORUS.	Greek: ARES.
Hebrew: ELOHIM GIBOR.	Archangel: KHAMAEL.
Roman: MARS.	Nordic: THOR.
Colour: ORANGE.	Attribute: RIGHT SHOULDER.
Metal: IRON.	Gemstones: RUBY.
Incense: GALANGAL.	Plants: NETTLE.
Titles: JUSTICE.	Number: 5.
Symbols: SWORD.	E.Q. value: 39.

Mars is the God of War and battles. His power when it is undirected is usually destructive, but when it is directed by the creative will it is the energy of labour.

Courage and justice are also Martial. He is the wielder of the Sword of Justice and he brings vengeance, dividing right from wrong. He is the Warrior of the Stars who gives force and energy – which used properly is constructive, though this may mean destroying what is old and worn to make way for the new. His power is invoked with care to bring energy and forcefulness; when in conjunction with another planet He unites His force with the blessings of the deity involved and thus energises and exaggerates its power.

The Greeks named Him Ares; to the Norsemen He was the mighty Thor. His Egyptian name is Horus, the Avenger. The Martial deity is always associated with war and vengeance, with courage and forcefulness.

In our natal charts Mars indicates our strength and force of character, and the way in which our energy is expressed and used. In ourselves He is represented by the right shoulder; His symbols are the sword, chain and scourge. The colours of Mars are orange and scarlet; His metal is iron, and the ruby is His particular gemstone. The incense is galangal and the plant ruled by Mars is the nettle.

JUPITER
♃

Egyptian: AMOUN.	Greek: JOVE.
Hebrew: EL.	Archangel: TZADKIEL.
Roman: JUPITER.	Nordic: WOTAN.
Colour: DEEP VIOLET.	Attribute: LEFT SHOULDER.
Metal: TIN.	Gemstones: AMETHYST, LAPIS LAZULI.
Incense: CEDAR.	Plants: OLIVE.
Titles: MERCY.	Number: 4.
Symbols: WAND, SCEPTRE.	E.Q. value: 143.

Jupiter is the God of Wealth and prosperity. His power is the constructive force of the perfection of the Supreme Will in action. He bears the Orb and Sceptre of a benign and merciful King and He brings riches spiritual and material to His worshippers. He is invoked conjunct the Moon when we desire an abundance of success and fulfilment of our plans, and in conjunction with another planet He equilibriates the power of the deity concerned into ordered harmonious joviality.

The Egyptians knew Him as Amoun the protector and preserver. To the Norsemen He was Wotan the

All-Father; the Greeks named Him Jove. Jupiter is always associated with the royal splendour of peaceful constructive government, with the stability and order of the Law-giver.

In our natal charts Jupiter reveals the nature and force of our religious and spiritual aspirations and influences our material wealth. In ourselves He is represented by the left shoulder. His symbols are the Orb and Sceptre, the Wand and the Crook; His colours are deep violet and blue, His gemstones are amethyst and lapis lazuli and tin is the metal sacred to Him. Cedar is the incense sacrificed to Jupiter and the olive is His particular plant.

PLANETARY FEASTS

IT IS THE custom in the O∴A∴A∴ to include an appropriate feast in our ritual celebrations; most often at the end, but sometimes as a timed interlude between two aspects either in the temple or in an appropriately decorated and furnished dining area, in which case we usually bring the thurible to the table. The more attention to detail the better, with table linen of the appropriate colour, and maybe table ornamentation in keeping with the deities invoked: roses for Venus, sea shells for the Moon, amethyst crystals for Jupiter, red candles for Mars, and so on.

Champagne is the alcoholic beverage of choice as it quickly imparts a sense of good fellowship and bonhomie to the assembly, and rarely incapacitates for any length of time, leaving the celebrants none the worse so long as they have consumed sufficient water as well, and quite capable of finishing a ritual ceremony.

It is relatively easy to develop a range of menus for all occasions. A basic rule is red meat for the Gods and white meat for the Goddesses. Dairy produce, most shellfish, and white food generally, belong to the Moon. Pork and chicken are Venusian, although chicken cooked in red wine would serve for the Sun; poultry mostly belongs to Venus except for pigeon and turkey which are Jupiterian. Oysters and mussels are obviously for Venus; and deep-sea creatures such as squid are Neptunian. Lamb is a Solar meat, while beef and venison are more appropriate to Jupiter; steak is for Mars, who also likes all hot and spicy foods. Mercury has food which cooks quickly; the Moon has root vegetables and rice and mushrooms; Venus has olives and pulses.

Dessert courses are similarly flexible. Cream and cheesecakes and pale-coloured fruit would serve the Moon. Venus likes honey, and figs, and apples, and almonds, and anything sweet. Gingerbread would be acceptable to Mars, while Jupiter would prefer something a bit heavier and richer, such as a gateau or even a trifle. Cinnamon and nutmeg are Solar flavours.

A menu for a Venus-Jupiter feast with secondary aspects to Mars, Mercury, and the Moon was as follows:

A spit-roasted chicken served on a large brass tray surrounded with kebabs, samosas, and little apple fritter-balls, and platters of focaccia bread made with black olives. The medieval style always seems appropriate to Jupiter, and so we dispense with cutlery. The brass tray, and the quick frying batter, fulfil the Mercurial correspondence, while the hot spices in the square-shaped samosas, and bell peppers and steak on the kebabs do the same for Mars and Jupiter. Venus and the Moon are represented in the chicken, the apple fritters, and the olive bread. For dessert there were slices of an almond croissant plait, choux pastry puffs, and a confection of dark and white chocolate with little pieces of crystallized ginger, orange peel, and macadamia nuts.

THE WEAPONS OF STELLAR MAGICK

THERE ARE FOUR weapons required in Stellar Magick – the Wand, Cup, Knife and Pantacle. Each weapon symbolises a different element: thus, the wand is the weapon of fire, the cup is the weapon of water, the pantacle is the weapon of earth, and the knife is the weapon of air. They represent different aspects of a force and also different ways of dealing with it. The fire wand directs power, the air knife can change its nature. The cup contains and the pantacle earths, each in a specific way.

The power invoked by the fire wand can be directed to negative symbols like the cup and pantacle. These negative weapons can then be charged with the planetary force. The method is to invoke the power from above via the Qaballistic Cross, and is directed down the wand through the right arm. The power is visualised in the colour appropriate to the planet involved. The magician visualises the force pouring down from the planet and suffusing him in its energy. It streams from the wand and charges the cup or pantacle with whatever energy is required by the ceremony.

The wand is used to invoke the powers of Jupiter, Mercury, and the Sun. The wand is a symbol of the will, as these planets are symbols of the divine will. The knife is used for banishings, for cutting parchment or paper, making pen-nibs, and so forth; and to invoke the powers of Mars, because the energy of Mars is so violent that only a destructive weapon can mediate it. It is a weapon to be used with care in Stellar Magick for works of destruction and vengeance where the magickian invokes the power of Mars at the astrologically correct moment, charges his knife with its power and stabs the symbol of his enemy. The symbol can be anything from a photographic image to a talisman. When a magician resorts to this kind of magic it is a very good idea that he make certain that he has not lost the golden thread. He must know that the law of Karma will cause him to experience that which he is afflicting on others. There is no grace and guilt in magic. The balance will be redeemed and that is all.

The cup is a wonderful weapon, it is owned by all of the Goddesses and he who knows how to wield it can be assured of the hearts of all real women. The cup is used to invoke the spirits of the Moon and Venus. The powers of Venus are truly visions of beauty. She is second only to Mars in ease of invocation. The spirits of these two planets can be conjured to visible appearance easily when their stars are right. The best way of dealing with the power of Venus is to hold the cup in the left hand, and allow the power to flow through it into the cup. I find it easier to use the Amber aspect of Her light than the emerald when charging a cup. The cup itself can be empty, or water or wine can be charged with Her power. This is useful if one wishes to influence a lady. However if the Goddess is simply invoked and worshipped this should be enough, without going to all the trouble of being specific and invoking her for a particular woman. If one is beloved of the Goddess she will give of her daughters with open arms: it is usually enough to invoke Venus to intercede on one's behalf. She is also, being the Goddess of beauty, the principle invoked for all works of art and beauty. The Moon is also invoked with the cup, for specific direction.

The Pantacle is usually made from a disk of white marble, or oak, or beeswax, and carries a simple cross within a circle. It represents the Earth, and our Path upon it, and the steadfastness of our Magickal Will, of which it is both the focal point and the foundation.

The weapons must be made or acquired and consecrated under the correct Stellar influences so that they vibrate in sympathy with and mediate the power involved. The ritual of the appropriate planet is used to consecrate the weapon. The weapons must be perfumed with the appropriate perfume and ideally kept in silks of the appropriate colour. The perfume must be blessed and consecrated on the feast day of the planet.

A preliminary consecration is performed in the day and hour of the planet. The Grand consecration is performed on the feast day of the planet which governs the weapon: we would use Sun conjunct Moon in Aries for the Wand; Sun conjunct Venus for the Cup; Sun conjunct Jupiter for the Pantacle; and Sun conjunct Mars for the Knife; using the invocations of the planets as indicated later on.

A burning incense stick is used to make the symbols over the weapon: there must be nothing left of the incense stick at the end of the rite so that the integrity of the weapon is preserved.

The Wand is of the element of Fire, and the incense used is galangal or camphor.

The Cup is of the element of Water, and the incense used is rose, sandalwood, and a tiny amount of vanilla.

The Pentacle is of the element of Earth, and the incense used is dittany mixed with cedar.

The Knife is of the element of Air, and the incense used is a general incense tinged with sulphur.

In the event of the weapons being unavailable, the Tarot Aces may be used since they represent the same forces.

PLANETARY TALISMANS

THE MANUFACTURE OF talismans depends for its effectiveness on the ability of the magickian to mediate the invoked planetary forces and direct the forces into a talisman. The material from which the talisman is made should vibrate in sympathy with the planet invoked. This can be a metal sacred to the planet or a more general purpose material such as parchment, hand-made paper or beeswax. Each material should be consecrated to the work.

Tradition requires that parchment should be from a new-born or very young animal, the reason being that the spirit of the animal contained within the parchment should be as pure as possible and therefore easily directed to the will of the planetary spirit invoked.

Hand made paper is usually made by the magician himself from a plant or material sacred to the planet invoked, while beeswax shares to a certain extent the nature of parchment with the added power that it partakes of all the spirits of nature, in that bees symbolise that crystallization in their mode of life and production of wax and honey.

These ideas, although somewhat obscure to the reasoning mind, have a logic that is the currency of the unconscious mind or Astral plane. Don't worry if you don't fully understand the whys and wherefores, your unconscious is structured in just the same way as everyone else's and will always respond in a magical way to a magical act.

Many other materials can, and have been used to make talismans. You will develop an instinct for this as you become more proficient in the art of Stellar magick.

For Solar conjunctions we would use the metal appropriate to the planet after first demagnetizing it of previous forces by heating it and exorcising influences from it. The *Key of Solomon* is recommended to the student desirous of more information on this subject. For lesser influences such as the Moon or mutual aspects we use beeswax or paper.

If it is desired to melt an old beeswax talisman down and re-use it, it must only be used for that planet's forces to which it had previously been dedicated. It would be extremely unwise to use material that had been dedicated to Saturn for Jupiterian purposes! Care must be taken when invoking a planetary power to do a specific task that the spirit invoked has authority over the task required of it. It is no use invoking a Mars spirit for material wealth, for it would only interpret "wealth" as great energy. Therefore one must make sure that one is invoking the right planetary spirit for the job. Also, great caution must be exercised in the making of Mars and Saturn talismans, as they are not easily destroyed once prepared. The talisman must be completely deconsecrated by ceremony, and demagnetized by heating.

The design of a planetary talisman is very much a matter for the individual magickian and the purpose for which it is intended.

BASIC RITUAL HOUSEKEEPING AND
TEMPLE ETIQUETTE

IT MAY NOT be possible to have a permanent Temple in a room designated for that purpose, nor even access to a space devoted to such an end and furnished with an altar, and the would be ritualist may have to adapt to his or her surroundings. However there are a few procedures which are customarily performed in some fashion in all magical ceremonies whether they be out of doors or in a dedicated Temple or in the office or in a corner of the bedroom. This will be familiar ground to the experienced occultist, but for those who are new to the game we will now include some of the very simple rules which in the O.'.A.'.A.'. we give to our new initiates.

It is appropriate to enter the Temple space, or to approach the Altar, from the North, whether it be a designated room, or a space within a room, or a situation out of doors. The gesture known as the Sign of the Rending of the Veil is made at the entrance; this Sign consists of taking one pace forward and making with both hands a movement as of opening a pair of curtains with arms outstretched at shoulder height. The Veil should be visualised as suspended between two pillars, and may be given a suitable colour and adorned with shapes, symbols, and so forth, according to the skill of the ritualist and the requirements of the ritual.

Once inside the Temple space we walk around it three times in a deosil or clockwise direction. This is done to raise consciousness. All movement within the Temple space should be in a clockwise direction until the end, when we will walk three times widdershins to return to normal consciousness before leaving. Then we will turn on the threshold of our temple space and make the Sign of Closing the Veil, followed by the Sign of Silence. These two Signs flow easily into each other, the first involving reaching out with both arms at shoulder height to draw the curtains closed, and then stepping back and placing one forefinger to the lips, letting the other arm hang straight down at the side with the fist lightly closed; and hold the pose for a moment. This sequence of opening and closing effectively encapsulates all that happens in between.

The Altar is usually positioned in the East, especially if it is large enough to be permanent. Some O.˙.A.˙.A.˙. members use a smaller Altar which they can place in the centre, or in the quarter corresponding to the significant planetary position: these are made in the traditional double cube shape and painted in black and white. The Altar is usually covered with altar cloth of the appropriate colours for the ritual. The Temple, (or, the Altar) should be arranged in advance, and if possible all will be in darkness when we enter, barefooted, with our hoods up if we are wearing robes, in which case we will doff them after the opening circumnambulations are complete, and put them back up again when we are ready to leave. Only the first to enter needs to give the Sign of the Rending of the Veil, and he or she should bless and light a candle on the Altar, whose flame is then used to light the other candles in the Temple; there should be no electric light unless it is unavoidable.

Banishings and purifications usually come next. A Lesser Banishing Pentagram Rite can be performed with the Knife or with a stick of incense which has been lit with a simple blessing such as the one given later on, and this will serve also to purify the place.

There are many variations and elaborations of these few simple habits, and much literature which deals with them at greater length. Further purifications by Fire and Water may be appropriate, followed by a Statement of Intent in which we will declare our purpose and ask for a blessing to sanctify our work; and other preliminary prayers. At the end it may be desirable to give a "License to Depart" to allow invoked spirits to leave, before closing the ritual.

These small observances are simply good magickal practice and serve to set the ritual and the space in which it is performed apart from the mundane world, a separation which is important for the integrity of the ritual and therefore a vital component of a successful outcome.

3. PRACTICE

Preliminary consecrations, planetary invocations,
invocations of Fortuna, planetary blessings,
License to Depart.

PRELIMINARY CONSECRATIONS

(CONSECRATION OF THE INCENSE:)

In the names of RAPHAEL, MICHAEL, GABRIEL, and AURIEL, I bless thee and integrate thee, o creature of earth, by this symbol (give Cross symbol), so that thou mayest be consecrated as a body for the spirits of (*) so that through thy earthly being the God (*) may manifest in the world.

(CONSECRATION OF THE FIRE:)

In the names of RAPHAEL, MICHAEL, GABRIEL, and AURIEL, I bless thee and integrate thee, o creature of fire, by this symbol (give Cross symbol), so that thou mayest be consecrated as a body for the spirits of (*) so that through thy fiery being the God (*) may manifest in the world. (Light incense.)

[(*): *here insert appropriate planetary name.*]

We would normally use this consecrated incense to perform a banishing as part of our opening and purification rites.

The simple formula employed here may easily be adapted for use with different Elements, Names, sigils, talismans, etc.

PLANETARY INVOCATIONS

THE FOLLOWING RITUALS from the O∴A∴A∴ archives are designed on Astro-Qaballistic lines for invocation of planets during periods of their greatest power. They are general purpose rituals in that they invoke the force and make it available to the ritualist. When some experience has been gained, the magickian may discover personal variations and additions to suit his development.

The rituals, by their construction and use of magical sounds cause a space in the time continuum where the magickian can impose his Will upon the moment and cause changes to occur in conformity with his Will, which is made the aim of all practical magick. The use of colour, sound, geometrical shapes, perfumes, etc, will according to the skill of the practitioner enhance and direct the forces in specific directions to produce a desired result.

As regards the drawing of the Planetary Hexagrams, begin at point 1, drawing an equilateral triangle in a clockwise direction. Then draw the second triangle (again clockwise) beginning at point 2. Whilst drawing the Hexagram, vibrate the word "ARARITA", and finally, inscribe the Planetary Glyph in the centre of the Hexagram, whilst vibrating the Hebrew God-Name associated with the planet.

In the case of the Sun, each of the other six Planetary Hexagrams are superimposed, therefore twelve triangles must be drawn, each beginning at the point indicated. The word "ARARITA" is to be vibrated once for each pair of triangles.

QABALLISTIC CROSS.

(The Cup is held in both hands to inscribe the Cross
as follows):

(Above head): In the Name of YHVH ALOAH-VE-
DAATH.

(Draw light down through central column to feet)

(Touching left shoulder): RAPHAEL.

(Draw light through to right shoulder): MALACHIM.

(Clasp hands about the flame before the breast): SOL – AMEN.

(The ritualist sets down the Cup and takes up the Wand,
holding it with both hands).

I invoke Thee SOL, Crowned and Mediating Lord
of the Stars. I invoke Thee in thy Highest and most
mysterious Name of Rose – YHVH ALOAH-VE-
DAATH. Permit me to partake of Thy Harmony in the
Golden Joy of RAPHAEL. Send me from among Thy
MALACHIM a Spirit to aid me in my work of Joy and
Harmony.

O Thou Beauteous One, I invoke Thee by Thy Symbols
of the Rose-Cross, the Lamen and the Cube. I invoke
Thy Spirits O YHVH ALOAH-VE-DAATH that I may
partake in the Harmony of Thy Love.

THE HEXAGRAM.

(Inscribed using the Wand in the right hand)

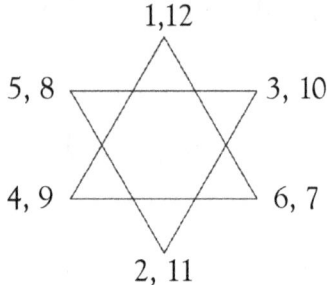

```
              1,12
               /\
              /  \
5, 8  _____/_____  3, 10
      \      \    /      /
       \      \  /      /
        \      \/      /
4, 9     \     /\     /   6, 7
          \   /  \   /
           \ /    \ /
            X      X
             \    /
              \  /
               \/
             2, 11
```

(Whilst inscribing the Hexagram, vibrate): ARARITA.

(Whilst inscribing the Glyph, vibrate): YHVH ALOAH-VE-DAATH.

Thee I invoke the Giver of Light.
Thee, that didst create the Pulse of Life.
Thee, that didst create the Brilliance and the Gold.
Thee, that didst create the Beauty and Harmony.
Thou art Ra, Helios, Apollo whom all men emulate.
Thou art King. Thou art the Priest.
Thou hast distinguished between the Form and the Force.
Thou didst make Integrity of Purpose.
Thou didst produce the Harmony of the Universe.
Thou didst form men to undergo thy ordeals in the Mystery of the Light.

QABALLISTIC CROSS

(The Cup is used to inscribe the Cross as above).

INVOCATION OF THE MOON

QABALLISTIC CROSS
(The Cup is held in both hands to inscribe the Cross
as follows):

(Above head): In the Name of SHADDAI-AL-CHAI.

(Draw light down through central column to feet)

(Touching left shoulder): GABRIEL.

(Draw light through to right shoulder): KERUBIM.

(Clasp hands about the flame before the breast): LUNA –
AMEN.

(The ritualist sets down the Cup and takes up the Wand,
holding it with both hands).

I invoke Thee LUNA, Crowned and Strong Queen of the
Stars. I invoke Thee in Thy Highest and most mysterious
Name of Indigo SHADDAI-AL-CHAI. Permit me
to partake of Thy Mystery in the Violet Strength of
GABRIEL. Reveal to me from among Thy KERUBIM a
Spirit to aid me in my work of Astral Magick.

O thou Strong One, I invoke Thee by Thy Symbols
of the Perfumes and Sandals. I invoke Thy Spirits
O SHADDAI-AL-CHAI that I may partake in the
Strength of Thy Magick."

THE HEXAGRAM.

(Inscribed using the Wand in the right hand)

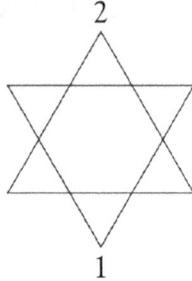

(Whilst inscribing the Hexagram, vibrate): ARARITA.
(Whilst inscribing the Glyph, vibrate): SHADDAI-AL-CHAI.
(The ritualist lays down the Wand and takes up the Cup, holding it aloft with both hands).

Thee I invoke, the Foundation of the World.
Thee, that didst create the Rhythm of Life.
Thee, that didst create a Mirror for the Universe.
Thee, that didst create the Flux and Reflux.
Thou art Astarte, Persephone, Diana, by whom all men are mystified.
Thou art Princess. Thou art the Queen.
Thou hast distinguished between that which is, and that which is to come.
Thou didst make the Astral and its Magic.
Thou didst produce the Time and its Finity.
Thou didst form men to penetrate Thy Mystery and partake of Thy Strength.

QABALLISTIC CROSS

(The ritualist inscribes the cross as above).

INVOCATION OF MERCURY

QABALLISTIC CROSS
(The whole ritual is performed with the wand).

(Above head): In the Name of ELOHIM TZABAOTH.

(Draw light down through central column to feet)

(Touching left shoulder): MICHAEL.

(Draw light through to right shoulder): BENI ELOHIM.

(Clasp hands about the flame before the breast): MERCURY - AMEN.

I invoke Thee MERCURY, Crowned and Winged Herald of the Stars. I invoke Thee in Thy Highest and most mysterious Name of Purple ELOHIM TZABAOTH. Permit me to partake of Thy Splendour in the Orange Truth of MICHAEL. Despatch to me from among Thy BENI ELOHIM a Spirit to aid me in my work of Truth and Intellect.

O thou Swift One, I invoke Thee by Thy Symbols of the Names, the Versicles and the Apron. I invoke Thy Spirits O ELOHIM TZABAOTH that I may partake in the Splendour of Thy Truth.

THE HEXAGRAM.

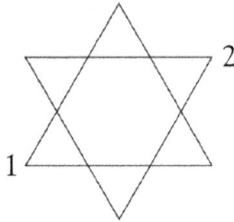

(Whilst inscribing the Hexagram, vibrate): ARARITA.

(Whilst inscribing the Glyph, vibrate): ELOHIM TZABAOTH.

Thee I invoke, the Lord of Reason.
Thee, that didst create number and order.
Thee, that didst create the Purple and the Orange.
Thee, that didst create Science and its Application.
Thou art Thoth, Hermes, Mercury, whom all men imitate.
Thou art the Monkey. Thou art the Jackal.
Thou hast distinguished between the True and the False.
Thou didst make Honesty of Purpose.
Thou didst produce the necessity for explanation.
Thou didst produce men to disseminate the Word forever.

QABALLISTIC CROSS
(The ritualist inscribes the cross as above).

INVOCATION OF VENUS

QABALLISTIC CROSS
(The Cup is held in the right hand to inscribe the Cross as follows):

(Above head): In the Name of YHVH TZABAOTH.

(Draw light down through central column to feet)

(Touching left shoulder): HANAEL.

(Draw light through to right shoulder): ELOHIM.

(Clasp hands about the flame before the breast): VENUS – AMEN.

(The ritualist lays down the Cup and takes up the Wand, holding it in the middle)

I invoke Thee VENUS, Crowned and Conquering Empress of the Stars. I invoke Thee in Thy Highest and most mysterious Name of Amber YHVH TZABAOTH. Permit me to partake of Thy Victory in the Emerald Beauty of HANAEL. Send me from among Thy ELOHIM a Spirit to aid me in my work of Beauty and Love.

O thou Beauteous One, I invoke Thee by Thy Symbols of the Rose, the Girdle and the Lamp of Illumination. I invoke Thy Spirits O YHVH TZABAOTH that I may partake in the triumph of Thy Beauty.

THE HEXAGRAM.

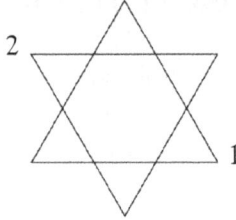

(The ritualist lays down the Wand and holds the Pantacle aloft with both hands)

Thee I invoke, The Beauteous One.
Thee, that dost adorn the Earth and The Heavens.
Thee, that art the Voluptuousness of Night and the Sensuality of Day.
Thee, that didst create the Love and the Beauty.
Thou art Venus, Aphrodite, Ahathoor whom all men desire.
Thou art Desire. Thou art the Object of Desire.
Thou hast distinguished between the Worthy and the Unworthy.
Thou didst make the Female and the Male.
Thou didst form men to adore Thine Image and partake of Thy Beauty.
Thou didst produce the Seed and the Fruit
Thou didst form men to love one another and hate one another.

THE ATTAINMENT.

I am She the Goddess of Love having Beauty as My Standard. Free and the Eternal Life.
I am She the Ecstasy.
I am She that caresses and inspires.
I am She from whom is the Love of the World.
I am She whose Beauty is everlasting .
I am She the Adornment and Sensuality of the Light.
I am She the Freedom of the Worlds.
The Light girt with Emerald is My Name.

THE CONSECRATION OF THE TALISMAN.

I adorn this talisman with the blessing of My Beauteous Spirit so that whomsoever possesses it shall be beloved by all who see it and consecrated to its possessor.

QABALLISTIC CROSS
(The Cup is used to inscribe the Cross as above).

INVOCATION OF MARS

QABALLISTIC CROSS
(The whole ritual is performed with the knife).

(Above head): In the Name of ELOHIM GIBOR.

(Draw light down through central column to feet)

(Touching left shoulder): KHAMAEL.

(Draw light through to right shoulder): SERAPHIM.

(Clasp hands about the flame before the breast): MARS – AMEN.

I invoke Thee MARS, Crowned and Conquering Warrior of the Stars. I invoke Thee in Thy Highest and most mysterious Name of Orange ELOHIM GIBOR. Permit me to partake of Thy Power in the Scarlet Courage of KHAMAEL. Command from among Thy SERAPHIM a Spirit to aid me in my work of War and Vengeance.

O Thou Mighty One, I invoke Thee by Thy Symbols of the Chain, the Scourge and the Sword of Justice. I invoke Thy Spirits O ELOHIM GIBOR that I may partake in the Power of Thy Courage.

THE HEXAGRAM.

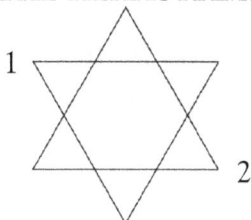

(Whilst inscribing the Hexagram, vibrate): ARARITA.

(Whilst inscribing the Glyph, vibrate): ELOHIM GIBOR.

Thee I invoke, the Terrible One.
Thee, that didst destroy the Weak and the Effete.
Thee, that didst destroy the Outmoded and Worn.
Thee, that didst create the Crimson and the Scarlet.
Thee, that didst create Battles and War.
Thou art Mars, Ares, Horus, whom all men fear.
Thou art the Warrior King. Thou art the God of Battle.
Thou hast distinguished between the Worthy and the Unworthy.
Thou didst make the Terror and Destruction.
Thou didst produce the Scourge and the Sword.
Thou didst form men to do battle with one another.

QABALLISTIC CROSS
(The ritualist inscribes the cross as above).

INVOCATION OF JUPITER

QABALLISTIC CROSS
(The whole ritual is performed using the wand).

(Above head): In the Name of EL.

(Draw light down through central column to feet)

(Touching left shoulder): TZADKIEL.

(Draw light through to right shoulder): CHASMALIM.

(Clasp hands about the flame before the breast): JUPITER – AMEN.

I invoke Thee JUPITER, Crowned and Throned King of the Stars. I invoke Thee in Thy Highest and most mysterious Name of Violet EL. Permit me to partake of Thy Majesty in the Royal Blue Glory of TZADKIEL. Bid me from among Thy CHASMALIM a Spirit to aid me in my work of Wealth and Majesty.

O Thou Magnificent One, I invoke Thee by Thy Symbols of the Orb, the Wand and the Sceptre of Thy Majesty. I invoke Thy Spirits O EL that I may partake in the Glory of Thy Prosperity.

THE HEXAGRAM.

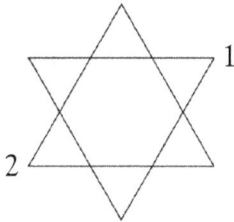

(Whilst inscribing the Hexagram, vibrate): ARARITA.

(Whilst inscribing the Glyph, vibrate): EL.

Thee I invoke, the Bounteous one.
Thee, that didst create the Wealth of Earth and the Joy of the Heavens.
Thee, that didst create the Purple and Gold.
Thee, that didst create Wealth and Abundance.
Thou art Jupiter, Zeus, Amoun, to whom all men aspire.
Thou art the King. Thou art the Emperor.
Thou hast distinguished between that which is, and that which is not.
Thou didst make the King and his Magic.
Thou didst produce the Gold and the Jewels.
Thou didst form men to partake of Thy Wealth and Thy Glory.

THE ATTAINMENT

I am He the Bounteous Spirit, having Glory as My Heart and Love of the Immortal Fire.

I am He the Joy.
I am He whose Glory is manifest in the World.
I am He the Laughter of the Universe.
I am He the Joy of the Life of Earth.
I am He whose mouth speaks the Glory.
I am He the King and Emperor of the Light.
I am He the Glory of the Worlds.
The Golden Orb and Bejewelled Sceptre is My Name.

THE CONSECRATION OF THE TALISMAN.

I bless this Talisman with the Spirit of Wealth and Prosperity so that whomsoever possesses it shall be blest with my Glory.

QABALLISTIC CROSS
(The ritualist inscribes the cross as above).

INVOCATIONS OF FORTUNA

Arise at dawn, and look toward the East.

Be still and quiet, and without strain become aware of the Sky. Relax your mind, let it be free to "be". Know that as the Part of Fortune is conjunct the moon so your personality has become a chalice for the Spirit of the cosmos. Allow yourself to become that chalice, raise your arms in the form of a 'V' toward the rising Sun so that the Grail may be completed by its light. Stand with your arms raised towards the rising Sun and feel the power of the Completed Grail entering your personality; and invoke:

"I adore thee, thou light of the world. I adore thee thou Light of the Grail, I ask nothing from thee for I am become thee. I and thee are one in the perfection of The Grail, the great mystery of our life."

(Look at the different colours of Dawn and let them enter your being so that by contemplation they may speak to your intuition and you may partake of their mystery.)

A simple daily Fortuna-Venus invocation may be performed as follows:

"I invoke thee thou great and beauteous Goddess, Venus, Hathoor, Aphrodite. I burn the incense to Thee. I invoke thee, thou Empress, Jehovah Tzabaoth. Come thou forth thou emerald Archangel, Hanael.

"Venus-Aphrodite, victorious Goddess! bring thy beauty and wonder into the lives of men, let Thy Love pour into our hearts from the Cup of Isis! I invoke Thy most glorious name, Thou Morning Star, Thou Beauty of the Stars, come thou forth and bless us with thy radiant light, made perfect in the Chalice of Heaven! Make all the spirits subject to Thy wondrous love, so that every spirit of the firmament and of the ether, upon the earth and under the earth, on dry land and in the water shall be conquered by Thy beauty, that they may be made whole by the eternal light of Thy Love."

With a lit incense stick make the Venus Hexagrams to the four Quarters, then above and below, thus invoking Venus into every aspect of experience.

End this simple invocation with 'So mote it be – Amen'.

PLANETARY BLESSINGS

SUN

If it be the Will of the Lord of Life and Change, may * receive the blessing of the Sun.

In the Name of JEHOVAH ELOAH VE DAATH and by the power of RAPHAEL, may the stellar influences in *'s life be harmoniously mediated and illuminate *'s heart with joyous love, that *'s intuition shall rule *'s affairs with compassion and the consciousness of the continuity of existence.

MOON

If it be the Will of the Lord of Life and Change, may * receive the blessing of the Moon.

In the Name of SHADDAI EL CHAI and by the Power of GABRIEL, may the foundation of *'s instinct be strengthened with discrimination, that the seeds of *'s dreams find fertile ground in which to flourish and bear fruit in harmony with the darkness and the light, according to Time and Season.

MERCURY

If it be the Will of the Lord of Life and Change, may * receive the blessing of Mercury.

In the Name of ELOHIM TZABAOTH and by the Power of MICHAEL, may *'s intellect be synthesised by the Light of Truth, that in its Glory the swiftness of *'s thoughts shall be inspired with honesty and clarity of knowledge to inform *'s words with the magic of success in accordance with *'s Will.

VENUS

If it be the Will of the Lord of Life and Change, may * receive the blessing of Venus.

In the Name of JEHOVAH TZABAOTH and by the Power of HANAEL, may *'s love be enlightened by victory, that the triumph of beauty shall imbue * with all-embracing love, uniting the divided and fulfilling *'s desires with beauteous sensuality, according to *'s Art.

MARS

If it be the Will of the Lord of Life and Change, may * receive the blessing of Mars.

In the Name of ELOHIM GIBOR and by the Power of KHAMAEL, may *'s courage be tempered with justice, that the energy of *'s labours shall be vigorous and win powerful success.

JUPITER

If it be the Will of the Lord of Life and Change, may * receive the blessing of Jupiter.

In the Name of EL and by the Power of TZADKIEL, may *'s prosperity be increased with richness, that the abundance of *'s wealth shall be benign and confer regal joviality.

SATURN

If it be the Will of the Lord of Life and Change, may * receive the blessing of Saturn.

In the Name of JEHOVAH ELOHIM and by the Power of TZAPHKIEL, may *'s understanding be graced with steadfastness, that *'s endurance shall be sustained and maintained with patience.

LICENSE TO DEPART

May any spirits here entrapped by my Work be now set free to return to their abodes, with the blessing of this Sign *(make Sign of Cross)*. So mote it be, Amen.

AFTERWORD

YOU DO NOT need to be a great astrologer nor well versed in the Hebrew Kabbalah to become a Stellar Magickian; any occult experience will be useful, but not essential to the successful application of the principles I have described here. You do not even need to know a great deal of English Qaballa – however, Stellar Magick used correctly will bring about changes which are more properly called spiritual experiences, permanent alterations of consciousness, or Initiations, and E.Q. greatly facilitates the integration into the psyche of such results.

Be that as it may, the benefits of astrological timing are easily attained and highly appropriate for all sorts of occasions and endeavours. In describing how to accomplish such ends I have tried to bear in mind that this might be one of the first occult books that you have read. Therefore I have included sufficient detail to make this book a complete presentation of Stellar Ritual Magick.

INDEX

A

B

C

V

W